T0324129

Cambridge Elements ≡

Elements in Publishing and Book Culture
edited by
Samantha Rayner
University College London
Leah Tether
University of Bristol

SELLING BOOKS WITH ALGORITHMS

Anna Muenchrath
Florida Institute of Technology

CAMBRIDGE
UNIVERSITY PRESS

Shaftesbury Road, Cambridge CB2 8EA, United Kingdom

One Liberty Plaza, 20th Floor, New York, NY 10006, USA

477 Williamstown Road, Port Melbourne, VIC 3207, Australia

314–321, 3rd Floor, Plot 3, Splendor Forum, Jasola District Centre, New Delhi – 110025, India

103 Penang Road, #05–06/07, Visioncrest Commercial, Singapore 238467

Cambridge University Press is part of Cambridge University Press & Assessment, a department of the University of Cambridge.

We share the University's mission to contribute to society through the pursuit of education, learning and research at the highest international levels of excellence.

www.cambridge.org
Information on this title: www.cambridge.org/9781009339698

DOI: 10.1017/9781009339704

First published 2024

A catalogue record for this publication is available from the British Library.

ISBN 978-1-009-33969-8 Paperback
ISSN 2514-8524 (online)
ISSN 2514-8516 (print)

Selling Books with Algorithms

Elements in Publishing and Book Culture

DOI: 10.1017/9781009339704
First published online: November 2024

Anna Muenchrath
Florida Institute of Technology

Author for correspondence: Anna Muenchrath, amuenchrath@fit.edu

ABSTRACT: In 1997 Amazon started as a small online bookseller. It is now the largest bookseller in the US and one of the largest companies in the world due, in part, to its implementation of algorithms and access to user data. This Element explains how these algorithms work, and specifically how they recommend books and make them visible to readers. It argues that framing algorithms as felicitous or infelicitous allows us to reconsider the imagined authority of an algorithm's recommendation as a culturally situated performance. It also explores the material effects of bookselling algorithms on the forms of labour of the bookstore. The Element ends by considering future directions for research, arguing that the bookselling industry would benefit from an investment in algorithmic literacy.

KEYWORDS: algorithms, bookselling, Amazon, readers, technology

ISBNs: 9781009339698 (PB), 9781009339704 (OC)
ISSNs: 2514-8524 (online), 2514-8516 (print)

Contents

Wise men contemplate the world, knowing full well that they are contemplating themselves.

—*Attributed to Fra Mauro and quoted in Robert Elliott Smith's* Rage Inside the Machine *(2019)*

Man is a creature who makes pictures of himself and then comes to resemble the picture. This is the process which moral philosophy must attempt to describe and analyze.

—*Iris Murdoch, quoted in Frank Pasquale's* The Black Box Society *(2016)*

The shamelessness of the rhetorical question "What do people want?" lies in the fact that it appeals to the very people as thinking subjects whose subjectivity it specifically seeks to annul.

—*Theodor Adorno and Max Horkheimer in* The Dialectic of Enlightenment *(1947)*

1 The Rise of Algorithms in Bookselling

In Jorge Luis Borges's 'The Library of Babel' (2007 [1941]), the universe, also known as the library, is made up of interminable, uniform hexagons each lined with five bookshelves on four walls (see Figure 1). Every shelf contains 35 books, every book 410 pages, every page 40 lines, and every line 80 letters. No two books are the same, and the organizing principle of the library, if there is one, is unknown. Many of the books, made up as they are of seemingly random variations of twenty-five orthographical symbols, simply comprise 'senseless cacophonies, verbal jumbles and incoherences' (53). Although it has not been found, it is speculated that one of the books must contain a faithful catalogue of the library. Following this logic, however, the library must also contain thousands of false catalogues. The inhabitants of this universe – its imperfect librarians – travel through the hexagons, stopping only to sleep standing up or to take care of biological necessities, searching for the one book that might make meaning of the library: a 'catalogue of catalogues'. Some go mad because the possibility of finding such a book 'can be computed as zero' (55).

Figure 1 A depiction of Borges's Universal Library created by Derek Philip Au using DALL-E 2, an AI system whose creators claim that it can 'create realistic images and art from a description in natural language'. See derekau .net/blog (16 July 2022).

If Borges's library were, instead, a bookstore I would hazard to guess that it would be uniquely unprofitable. Although readers in a bookstore might hope to browse the shelves in search of a special book, to do so for a lifetime would mean delaying the moment of sale beyond what would be practicable for the bookstore owner, who, after all, must eat and pay rent.

Imagine now that the hexagons of Borges's story are each outfitted with a small console, equipped with a search bar. Entering a string of letters produces a list of books featuring that string along with their locations in the universal library. This might eliminate some of the frustration of the inhabitants of the library, but it would ruin the story, which tells us that in our (desperate) search for knowledge it's never clear exactly what we're looking for or how to know that we've found it.

This Element is about how algorithms, and particularly search and recommendation algorithms, affect the acts of bookselling and book buying. Although algorithms exist across different phases of book production and consumption and are implemented in both online and brick-and-mortar bookstores, this Element focuses on the rise of Amazon.com, now the largest bookseller in the US, and its use of algorithms in recommending books to readers. This Element is not directly interested in the distinction between selling ebooks and physical books, or the rise of self-publishing, which has taken place inter alia on Amazon's Kindle Direct Publishing platform. It also brackets the role of algorithms on platforms like YouTube and Instagram that influence the sale of books through marketing (see Fuller and Sedo, 2023). Instead, this Element asks what is at stake for book buyers and sellers when readers take recommendations from bookselling algorithms online.

A Very Brief History of Bookselling in the US

Starting in the late 1960s, bookstores in the US began changing. Books had been sold in one-off, independent stores owned by local booksellers near the centre of towns, cities, and neighbourhoods, but they now moved off main street towards the growing malls and shopping centres. Following trends in other retail sectors, bookstores began capitalizing on their new, high-traffic locations by rationalizing stock management, which meant increasing stock turnover and stocking only books with a high likelihood of selling quickly (Thompson, 2010).

By the 1980s, these efforts were aided by rapid technological changes that increased efficiencies in predicting sales and turning over stock (Miller, 2006). These computerized systems, which recommended to booksellers what books to stock and for how long worked best at scale, and bookstore chains proliferated, taking the place of previously independent stores. Whereas the independent stores had been shaped by the knowledge and interests of individual booksellers and their understanding of the communities in which they operated, chains often featured the same, fast-selling titles across their locations. A chain store in one US mall was likely to feature much the same stock as the same chain store in a mall across the country (Thompson, 2010).

The proliferation of the chains came to a head in the 1990s with the rise of superstores. In 1992, the retail giant Kmart bought Borders, which had itself bought the bookstore chain Waldenbooks in 1984. Under Kmart's ownership, Borders and Waldenbooks merged to form Borders Group, which went public in 1995 and began to compete with the other superstore chain, Barnes & Noble. In the late 1990s, Borders and Barnes & Noble dominated the bookselling scene, outselling their closest rivals, the chain bookstores Crown and Books-a-Million, by a factor of anywhere from five to ten (Thompson, 2010). Like the chains, these superstores were able to maximize margins with computerized stocking systems, but they were also able to stock far more books in their super-sized footprints, which made them attractive to consumers looking for a one-stop book-buying experience.

This boom of nationwide bookstore chains and the competition they produced increased the availability of a large selection of books to more US Americans than ever before. The cost, however, was a decrease in independent bookselling. By the end of the millennium, chains accounted for over 50 per cent of book sales, while the sales of independent bookstores fell from 24 per cent of total book sales at the start of the 1990s to around 16 per cent by the decade's end. By 2006, independent bookstores made up about 13 per cent of total book sales in the US (Thompson, 2010). As the growth of the superstores slowed and even regressed in the first decade of the twenty-first century, the total number of bookstores began to fall. Although US Census Bureau figures (quoted in Miller, 2011, p. 18) tend to undercount totals, their numbers of dedicated bookstores dropped from 12,363 in 1997 to 9,955 in 2007. Of the 905 bookstores that closed between 2002 and 2007, 764 were independent stores with only one location. It is in this context that Amazon.com started selling books online.

The Emergence of Amazon

Amazon first started selling books online in 1995. Originally this was a very low-cost proposition. All it required was a website, packing materials, and use of the postal service. Customers went online and ordered books through Amazon.com, which were shipped to founder Jeff Bezos's small team from a wholesaler. The team then repackaged the books into customers' orders and sent them off. When Amazon went public in 1997, investors flocked to the offering, injecting large amounts of capital into the startup even though it had not yet shown signs of profitability. As sales increased, Amazon built its own distribution infrastructure, which allowed for quicker shipping times (Miller, 2006). As with the rise of the superstore chains, Amazon was increasing access to books (for customers with credit cards and internet access), and, for customers who didn't need their books right away, it increased the convenience of the purchase by not even requiring them to leave their homes. Although the book superstores had already made books much more widely available, Bezos's focus was on further expanding selection. Amazon.com provided, as Bezos writes in his 1997 shareholder letter, 'much more selection than was possible in a physical store (our store would now occupy 6 football fields)' available in 'a useful easy-to-search, and easy-to-browse format in a store open 365 days a year, 24 hours a day' (Bezos, 1997).

Why did what is now called *the everything store*, start out as a dedicated bookstore? Laura Miller (2006) points out that a history of successful mail-order sales demonstrated that buyers didn't need to handle books before purchasing them. Plus, Amazon was able to easily adopt *Books in Print* as its catalogue, transforming Bowker's indexical codex into a scrollable and searchable database. Books are relatively uniform in size, making the shipping and distribution process standardizable and inexpensive. As Matthew Kirschenbaum (2021, p. 81) writes, there is nothing logistically distinctive about books: they are 'amenable to just the kind of modularization supply chains demand'.

Although these factors all point to books' interchangeability (as John Thompson (2021, p. 143) notes 'a copy of a book was the same as another copy of the same book regardless of where you bought it'), books were a good testing ground for e-commerce because of the large number of distinct titles. Fortuitously, despite their diversity, books already came pre-stamped with individual International Standard Book Numbers (ISBN), which made them easily trackable. Mark McGurl (2021a) writes that in choosing books as its proto-product, Amazon was taking advantage of the fact that reading for pleasure was a pastime afforded to precisely the population that was most likely to have access to a credit card and an internet connection.

The choice of books then was, as Thompson (2021, p. 143) writes, not related to a desire to 'participate in and contribute to the culture of the book'. Books were simply well-suited to maximize the potential for rapid growth at the start of the e-commerce boom. Yet McGurl (2021a, pp. xii, xix) suggests that books represent a choice more meaningful than this narrative reveals, and that Amazon's start as a bookstore is embedded in and central to its commitment to 'facilitat[e] our access to fiction in various ways'. This fiction manifests itself in Amazon's authorship of 'an epic narrative' that follows 'the speedy satisfaction of popular want'. We can see the opening of this narrative written into the 1997 shareholder letter, where Bezos contends that although it is 'Day 1 for the Internet . . . .. Tomorrow, through personalization, online commerce will accelerate the very process of discovery'.

The idea of accelerating the process of discovery through personalization is something I'll return to in section 3. For now, we'll turn to the more banal yet monumental acceleration of Amazon's growth through the start of the twenty-first century. In 1995, Amazon's revenues were half a million dollars. This rose to $16 million in 1996, its second full year of business. In 1997, Barnes & Noble started competing with Amazon for online book sales. Despite this, Amazon became, in just three and a half years, the country's third largest bookseller behind Barnes & Noble and Borders (Hennessey, 2000, p. 39). The company, though, remained unprofitable, posting huge losses along with its mega-sales numbers. Kept aloft by shareholders and investors, the company focused on Bezos's motto: 'get big fast'. And it did. Amazon first became profitable in 2007. By 2010 Amazon's media sales, which include sales of books as well as sales of TV shows, music, and digital downloads, were $6.88 billion and growing rapidly. The sales of its closest competitor Barnes & Noble, were under $4.55 billion and falling (Thompson, 2021, p. 145).

Although it was launched as an online bookstore, Amazon steadily increased its retail offerings and by 2014 only 7 per cent of its revenue came from books (a number that has likely fallen since). That 7 per cent, however, constitutes roughly half of all US book purchases and 70 per cent of all ebook purchases (McGurl, 2016; Greco, 2019; Thompson, 2021). A SWOT analysis, created by an independent firm usually in the service of investors, is an overview of a company's strengths, weaknesses, opportunities, and threats. A recent SWOT analysis (Marketline, 2022) of Barnes & Noble lists as its major competitors Amazon.com, Books-A-Million, Costco, Target and Walmart. A SWOT analysis of Amazon, which grew

21.7 per cent in 2022 due to increased sales and the promotion of Amazon Web Services (AWS), a cloud-computing platform used by companies like Coca-Cola, Netflix, and BMW, doesn't even mention Barnes & Noble as a notable threat (Marketline, 2023).

These numbers are all to say that Amazon has become in the last few decades a powerful if not the most powerful player in the bookselling industry in the US. It has become the single most important customer of many university presses and small publishers, and one of the two or three largest accounts for the large trade publishers. The norms Amazon has introduced, such as free shipping, short delivery times, and extreme discounting, have put pressure on publishers and booksellers to fall in line or risk losing customers (Thompson, 2021).

Although I have framed Amazon's rise here in terms of the history of bookselling in the US, Amazon's effects on bookselling have also been global in scope. Amazon has major fulfilment operations in thirteen countries and distributes books and other products to customers in at least 150 countries. Amazon's newest successful venture, AWS, which has clients in 190 countries (McGurl, 2021a), draws on Amazon's experience in distribution: both cloud computing and global logistics are only profitable at a large scale. In the UK, whose bookselling history closely parallels that of the US with Waterstones and Dillons standing in for Barnes & Noble and Borders, Amazon is a major player (Thompson, 2021), as it is in many other countries, particularly in Europe and Canada.

Amazon's Algorithms

How is Amazon so effective and competitive at selling books online? Consider this anecdote furnished by David Sumpter:

> When I look at the books suggested for my favorite authors, the recommendations are spot on. Either I already own the book, or it is one I would like to get my hands on. During the two hours I just spent on Amazon's website 'researching' their algorithms, I ended up putting seven items in my basket. The algorithm understood not just me, but also my wife and my

relatives. I just did all my Christmas shopping in one sitting.
It even understands my teenage daughter better than I do:
when I looked up Dodie Clark's book *Obsessions, Confessions
and Life Lessons* it suggested that Elise might also like *Turtles
All the Way Down* by John Green. I am sure she will.

When I read fiction, I hear another person's words in my
own voice. It was a very personal experience, a social connection between me and the writer. Sometimes when I am
deep in a good novel, I believe that no other person will ever
talk to me in the way this writer has talked to me.

A few hours on Amazon dispels this illusion entirely.
(2018, p. 106)

This anecdote highlights several of the tensions produced in our interactions with algorithms that this Element will probe. Sumpter sees the
personalized recommendations offered on Amazon's site as uncannily
accurate. They mirror his existing purchasing habits by offering him
books he has already bought or books he plans to buy. As a professor of
applied mathematics, Sumpter is not perplexed by how Amazon achieves
this; he knows that there are algorithms working to produce the site as he
sees it real time, hoping to increase his purchases. Despite this, it works. He
accepts many of these recommendations, purchasing several of the items.
And not only do these algorithms seem to understand Sumpter, but they
also provide him with recommendations for others, such as his teenage
daughter. Sumpter is confident in this algorithmic recommendation; he is
sure his daughter will enjoy the book. All of this is extremely convenient.
His Christmas shopping is done in one sitting.

Literature, as Sumpter notes, can also feel personalized. It hails readers
as subjects of its fiction: a story cannot really exist in the world without the
active participation of a reader. Algorithms, as I'll argue in the next section,
are similar in that they are texts that cannot operate without the input of
users. Both our reading of literature and our interaction with algorithms, as
Sumpter notes, seem to reflect our subjectivity back to us. Sumpter's few
hours on Amazon dispel for him the uniqueness of the connection afforded
by literature by seemingly replicating that connection easily and repeatedly

with every click of his mouse. To what extent is this the case? What do we gain and what do we lose by accepting algorithms' instant recommendations? These are the questions that this Element aims to address.

If Sumpter's account is credible, Amazon's algorithms are effective at selling books, and, among factors like a huge selection, incomparable convenience, and competitive prices, are part of what has set Amazon apart as a bookseller. Amazon's product recommendation system was one of the first modern algorithms 'deployed at scale for consumers', as Mikhael Bhaskar (2020, p. 16) writes enthusiastically: 'books were in the vanguard!' As early as 2008, Amazon used eighteen different types of recommender systems on its website (Knotzer, 2008). Although the goal of this Element is to elucidate the effects of algorithms on bookselling, it is the case that we can't be sure what proportion of Amazon's success is attributable to its data collection and use of algorithms. However, the selling of books with algorithms is part of what Amazon itself calls the 'flywheel' or self-reinforcing loop that powers its business: lower prices lead to more customer visits, more customer visits lead to more sellers, which, in turn, lowers the relative fixed costs of fulfilment centres and servers (Stone, 2013, p. 98). Amazon's aim is to accelerate the flywheel, and technologies like the 'buy now' button or the outputs returned by search and recommendation algorithms decrease friction, lubricating the flywheel.

Although Amazon has had incredible impacts in the world of bookselling, Bezos himself calls it 'a technology company at its core' (quoted in Striphas, 2010, p. 303). This is why Amazon's closest competition is not Barnes & Noble. Instead, it is listed as one of the GAFAM/BATX companies, which is an acronym referring to Google, Apple, Facebook, Amazon, Microsoft, and Baidu, Alibaba, Tencent, and Xiaomi. In 2022, the Forbes Global 2000 list of the largest publicly traded companies had Apple seventh, Google (Alphabet) eleventh, Microsoft twelfth, Alibaba thirty-third, Tencent twenty-eighth, and Facebook (Meta) thirty-fourth. Amazon was sixth (Murphy and Contreras, 2022). Like these other companies, Amazon, although not invested in the culture of the book, is primarily concerned with, as Ted Striphas writes, 'delegating the work of culture – the sorting, classifying and hierarchizing of people, places, objects, and ideas – to data-intensive computation processes' (2015, p. 396). How, then, might this delegation of bookselling affect what we read?

The primary hurdle toward answering this question is the challenge of any inquiry into the functioning of proprietary algorithms, namely that on a technical level, their operations are hidden from public view. 'Who are', Frank Pasquale (2016, p. 80) asks, 'the men behind the curtain, and how are their black boxes sorting and reporting our world?' Employees of companies that rely on proprietary algorithms are often made to sign confidentiality clauses that prohibit them from disclosing algorithmic inputs (Marcus, 2010). However, even if the code of these algorithms were made public, it is unlikely that they would be easily comprehensible to even the most technically minded researcher. Nick Seaver (2017, p. 3) suggests that because these algorithms are usually collective products, no single coder has an overview of the whole. He quotes a senior software engineer at a music streaming platform: 'It's very much black magic that goes on in there; even if you code a lot of it up, a lot of that stuff is lost on you'. Here, the 'black box' becomes 'black magic', pointing up the opacity of algorithms, even to those who work most closely with them. Rob Kitchin (2017, p. 21) agrees that it is 'unlikely that any one programmer has a complete understanding of a system'.

In this Element, therefore, I follow the lead of several interdisciplinary forays into algorithmic critique that establish that knowing algorithms' code is not a necessary condition for critiquing their outputs and impacts. Safiya Umoja Noble (2018), for example, compares critiquing algorithms without knowing their code to interrogating song lyrics or television shows without understanding the mechanism of radio transmission or cathode ray tubes. Karl Berglund (2021, p. 140) agrees, adding that exaggerating the importance of the function of individual algorithms might 'mystify algorithms in the cultural industries even further'. And mystification will become a repeated refrain in what is to follow, particularly how algorithmic recommendations mystify our own preferences even as they mirror them back to us.

In the next section, I discuss what algorithms are: how they combine data and an understanding of the world based on probabilities to produce outputs that are necessarily ideologically freighted, and how machine learning implicates users as co-authors in the production of algorithmically processed data.

Section 3 focuses more specifically on the types of search and recommendation algorithms found on Amazon's site, and the impacts of personalization and collaborative filtering on bookselling. While algorithms appear to make previously invisible books visible, section 4 considers the types of labour that selling books with algorithms renders invisible. Section 5 concludes by briefly considering where an increased understanding of algorithmic recommendations in bookselling leads us, as well as some potential directions for future inquiry.

2 What Are Algorithms?

Algorithms are sets of procedures that operationalize the completion of a task. Imagine you are a bookseller, and you need to decide which books you should stock in the limited high-visibility shelves and tables of your store. You might consider the attractiveness of the covers, the anticipated popularity of the titles, as well as how much press or buzz each of the books has already received. You also might take into consideration what has sold well in the past, as well as your sense of the preferences of your regular customers. The profit margins on each book might come into play, as would any marketing agreements you have with publishers to feature certain titles prominently. Whether consciously or not, you would weigh a mixture of these inputs to make your selection. Algorithms, in the way we think of them working on a computer, can take inputs like these, rapidly complete an operationalized procedure, and produce a 'best' result, where 'best' is determined by the setting of pre-programmed goals (Gillespie, 2016).

Algorithms often simulate or stand in for human judgment, which is why they are also called automated decision systems (Richardson, 2021). They formalize the process of weighing multiple inputs to get effective answers, but they do so in a way that is automated and, once algorithms have been set up, relatively autonomous so that the decision can be made 'instantly, repetitively, and across many contexts, away from the guiding hand of [an algorithm's] implementers' (Gillespie, 2016, p. 26). To do this, the relevant inputs need to be turned into measurable data. Since algorithms cannot get a sense of, for example, how a store's regular customers have been responding to recent book displays (perhaps through increased traffic, body language, or comments to the bookstore staff), a dataset would need to be created to measure this type of interest, such as time spent viewing displays. However, it is more likely that a proxy for this data, like the number of purchases made from the display, would be used. As Robert Elliott Smith (2019, p. 151) writes, algorithms are always models of reality, representing a 'narrowing of scope to a particular concern,' which is then quantified, 'with an enumerated set of features'. Especially when it comes to human beings and human societies, these models are always simplifications because the number of factors at work make the problems 'combinatorially explosive', meaning that each additional factor exponentially increases the computing power required to calculate an output.

Although the great advantage of algorithms is that they operate automatically and outside of the supervision of humans, humans are responsible for deciding what data or data proxies are relevant, how to outline the steps of the problem, and what instructions to offer the program in choosing which output is 'best'. So, even though algorithms are intended to automate human decisions, in reality 'a great deal of expertise, judgement, choice and constraints' are required in their creation (Kitchin, 2017, p. 18). Although I'll return in a moment to the interactions between algorithms and their users, here we can already see that algorithms, despite appearing as a 'black box', are socio-technical assemblages (Gillespie, 2014; Ananny, 2016; Beer, 2017; Kitchin, 2017; Seaver, 2022; Striphas, 2023), collaborations between human coders, data, code, and the priorities of the corporations funding their development. Algorithms, as Seaver (2022, p. 6) writes, 'are full of people making decisions, changing things around, and responding to a never-ending stream of small and large crises .... Human actions are woven into the functioning of algorithms continually'. As new data is made available, scandals make the use of possibly flawed data unadvisable, or changing cultural values mean previous 'best' results are no longer 'best', algorithms are tweaked and adjusted by their minders to provide updated outputs.

The Algorithmic Imaginary and Performative Algorithms

I have somewhat belaboured the obvious involvement of human actors in setting up the parameters of algorithms because this involvement troubles the binary between the subjective decision-making of humans and the computational objectivity implicated in cultural imaginings of how algorithms work. It is safe to say that many people, especially those who interact with the internet frequently, are aware of their interactions with algorithms on search engines or social media sites, even if they cannot say precisely how they work or what effect they have their own actions. This is what Striphas (2023, p. 3) calls 'algorithmic imagination': 'instances in which people become aware of, and possibly self-reflexive about, their relationships to computationally based decision system', and what Taina Bucher (2018, p. 113) calls the 'algorithmic imaginary', which describes the 'ways of thinking about what algorithms are, what they should be, how they function'. This algorithmic imagination or imaginary is not always grounded in the reality of how algorithms work or are made, but it is often as important or even more so in determining how algorithms and their outputs are used, regarded, and regulated (or not) as automated decision systems that make (in concert with their human users) decisions that we would regard as cultural work, like bookselling.

Perhaps the most common fallacy of the algorithmic imaginary is a belief in algorithmic objectivity (Smith, 2019), also known as 'automation bias' (Bridle, 2018, p. 40), which is an effect that has been measured, for example, in pilots, who when studied tended to trust machine outputs rather than their own sense of reality. This belief is rooted in the idea that because algorithms must make 'rational' computations using numeric data they cannot be biased or subjective. Algorithmic selection becomes preferable to human selection because it is made using a quantitatively derived image of the world, rather than an impression of reality as subjectively interpreted by a human. In this imagining, algorithms circumvent and rationalize the bias and subjectivity of human selection procedures, and any attempt to intervene in them would disrupt this ability, introducing fallibility. This view, which rhymes with the invisible but purportedly correct logic of a free market economy, has been summarily debunked by data scientists and scholars of computer science (see, among many others, Burrell, 2016; O'Neil, 2016; Noble, 2018; Sumpter, 2018; Smith, 2019; Seaver, 2022), who show that the collection of data, the set-up of problems, the choice of problem, and the valuing of particular outputs are always already a function of the human concerns that make algorithms possible. Although algorithms 'deliver results with a kind of detachment, objectivity, and certainty', they ultimately reflect the preferences and priorities of the human cultures that create the logics on which they operate (Ananny, 2016, p. 97).

This is not to say that algorithms are wrong or false. It is just to say that the results algorithms present us with are not objective or free of bias, and, as Gillespie (2014, p. 175) writes, we would have no way of measuring whether or not they are since we usually have no 'unbiased judgment' with which we can compare an algorithmic output like a recommendation. This, though, is perhaps a boon to book recommendation algorithms, since what we are likely looking for in a recommendation is not objective (a measure, e.g., of the best book), but rather subjective – a sense of what we might *like*.

As we go about accepting an algorithmic book recommendation, we should be thinking not only about what algorithms are doing, but also how their outputs are being presented rhetorically and how that might influence the weight we (in our own, subjective algorithmic procedures) give them. Jonathan Cohn (2019, p. 22) suggests, for example, that the marketing surrounding algorithms may be more important than the recommendation itself, since, even when they aren't producing apt results, they continue to provide the appearance of 'luxury, care, and personal relationships'. On Amazon.com recommendations appear under a few different headings like 'Frequently bought together', which implies knowledge of other buyers, 'Products related to this item', which implies knowledge of this book and similar ones, 'Four Stars and Above', which attributes knowledge of books to other Amazon users who have rated other books, or 'Based on your recent views', which implies knowledge of you, the user. These types of recommendations, which often provide left-to-right scrollable outputs imitating the feeling of standing at a bookstore shelf, afford a sense of an efflorescence of personal relationships – between you and other users, and even between you and yourself – facilitated by the work of algorithms.

I propose, then, that rather than thinking of algorithmic outputs and especially recommendations as true or false, we adopt J. L. Austin's (1981) verbiage for what he calls performative utterances – utterances which he provisionally contrasts with constative statements (true or false descriptions of the world), and whose uttering is in fact the doing of the action described in the utterance. In the case of a marriage, for example, to say 'I do', is not just to say 'I do', it is also to complete the act of marriage. Of course, there are many caveats to the successful performative utterance. Saying 'I do' outside of a marriage ceremony, saying it in a marriage ceremony if you are already married, or saying it in a marriage ceremony with a monkey (all Austin's examples), mean, not that the statement is false, but rather that it is *infelicitous* – it hasn't really gone off. The statement being *felicitous* or *infelicitous* depends not only on the proposition itself but on the surrounding cultural situation in which the statement is uttered. The concept of felicity seems particularly apt for algorithms since, as Friedrich Kittler says, code is the only language that also does what it says (quoted in Galloway, 2006, p. 5).

What the idea of felicitous and infelicitous (rather than correct or incorrect) algorithmic recommendations affords us is to be able to think through some of Austin's conditions for felicity, and probe whether a given algorithmic recommendation meets them. For example, Austin (1981, p. 9) argues that in order for an utterance to be felicitous it must be spoken in seriousness, not in jest or as part of a poem; the 'outward utterance' is in this case 'a description, *true or false*, of the occurrence of the inward performance'. To ascertain whether the statements 'I do' or 'I bet that. . .' have been felicitous, we need to assess whether the statement is authentic to the inward feelings, thoughts, and intentions of the speaker. But how can we assess the 'inward performance' of algorithms? What would it mean for an algorithmic recommendation to be authentic or inauthentic? On the one hand, algorithms *cannot* be inauthentic; they must follow the dictates of their code. On the other hand, algorithms may present unpredictable results due to faulty data input, unanticipated feedback loops, or miscoding (Kitchin, 2017), which don't align with the intentions of their creators. In this case, we should likely not take their recommendation 'seriously'.

Another potential source of infelicity is the failed acknowledgement and, thereby, completion of the act by a speech partner. If you say 'I bet that. . .' but I don't take your bet, or if you say 'I do' but sadly your prospective spouse declines, the speech act has not been felicitous. 'The question', Austin (1981, p. 37) asks, 'is how far can acts be unilateral?' Imagine entering a bookstore and the bookseller, whom you've never seen before, is waiting by the door. Upon your entrance, she immediately starts listing books you might like. You did not ask for a recommendation, and you don't know how she's coming up with these titles. You would probably quickly exit the store, and you might consider these recommendations infelicitous in that they are unilaterally imposed – you did not agree to take a recommendation or ask for one.

Although performative utterances are often in the first person ('I bet. . .') they can also be made in the second or third person, as well as in the passive voice. Austin's (1981, p. 57) examples here are 'You are hereby authorized to pay. . .' and 'Passengers are warned to cross the track by the bridge only'.

As Austin notes in his examples, there is still an implicit 'I' here, who is essentially 'signing off' on the speech act: '(I advise/recommend that these are) products related to this item'. In the statement 'I hereby open this library', the utterance is not felicitous if the 'I' opening the library has not been endowed with the power to do so; instead, the library, to the chagrin of hopeful patrons, remains closed. A question we might ask is: in the statement 'I advise that these are books that you may like', who has endowed algorithms with the power to recommend? If you accept the recommendation, then we might answer that *you* have.

We'll return to these opportunities for infelicity – the authenticity of algorithms' inward performance, unilateral recommendations, and algorithms' authority to recommend – throughout the Element. For now, let's adopt the language of the felicitous recommendation as we consider what's at stake in accepting it.

There is a sense in the algorithmic imaginary that the felicity of a recommendation means that algorithms know or understand you. We saw this in Sumpter's (2018, p. 106) description of his interaction with Amazon's algorithms, which 'understood not just [him], but also [his] wife and [his] relatives'. There is a sense of validation when algorithms' results line up with your understanding of the world, when 'your pet topic trends on Twitter, when Amazon recommends a book you already love, or when Apple iTunes' 'Genius' function composes an appealing playlist from your library of songs' (Gillespie, 2014, p. 186). There are seemingly just as many occasions when algorithms provide you with a bizarre recommendation – a song that you actively despise, or a book that it should know you would never read. As Terje Colbjørnsen (2018, p. 177) finds in his research on responses to algorithmic recommendations, reactions often swing from 'the algorithm knows me better than I know myself' to 'go home algorithm, you're drunk'. The felicity of algorithmic recommendations seems to depend primarily on the user's understanding of themselves and whether the recommendation confirms that view or undermines it.

This very human response to algorithmic recommendation is repeated by Seaver, who uses an anthropological approach to ask how engineers and coders working on music recommendation algorithms view them. While shadowing an engineer who is working to build recommendation algorithms that will model and group music into genres, Seaver finds that when the output produced by these algorithms connects music that intuitively seems to be of a kind, Seaver and the engineer feel affirmed, but don't discuss the results; however, when these algorithms model the data in a way that provides them with an unexpected grouping, they begin trying to decipher what it is doing and why. 'The interpretability' of the output, Seaver (2022, p. 113) writes, is 'a consequence of our pre-existing knowledge and frames of reference. Ironically, situations that seem at first to be uninterpretable produce a wild efflorescence of interpretive work .... When an output is interpretable, it feels like it requires no interpretation at all'. Algorithmic outputs become an occasion for interpretation only when they undermine the cultural logics (here, of genre) familiar to Seaver and the engineer. Algorithms, in this case, are valuable not because they have an objective perspective, but because they offer us a new perspective on ourselves – a perspective that we perhaps intuitively seek to interpret.

Data, Information Capital, and Proxies

This perspective is derived from algorithms' assimilation of vast amounts of data, which they require to operate. The function of recommendation algorithms is essentially predictive. They use the data they have to extrapolate a prediction for a data point that doesn't yet exist. In early recommendation algorithms, the data was often explicit. Users would provide ratings for a set of products, and, by accessing a model of how those products related to one another, algorithms would predict a user's rating for a product he or she had not yet rated. As online data collecting became more robust, algorithms were able to use implicit ratings or data proxies: clicking and scrolling on certain parts of the site, spending time on one page over another, stopping/rewatching a video, or listening to a song multiple times. By tracking users through cookies, IP addresses, and browser and device profiles, platforms like Amazon build profiles of users that replace traditional market demographics with individual user preferences (Bridle, 2018).

Rather than relying on users to make a self-conscious assessment of what they like or don't like, this type of data is generally produced, mostly unknowingly, by users as they go about their online business. It is also, according to engineers of algorithms, more trustworthy. Users are more likely to dissemble in public ratings, claiming that they found *War and Peace* to be a five-star novel, when they have never read it and would not click on nor buy recommendations based on a book's similarity with it. But activity logs are harder to falsify. Engineers have also found that there is a natural limit to predictive accuracy when tracking user ratings since user ratings are themselves variable. If your rating for *War and Peace* varies from day to day or year to year, then algorithms using that rating are set up for failure. Furthermore, researchers have found that increasing the accuracy of the predicted rating for a given product doesn't always lead to user satisfaction; in other words, users don't always want to be recommended items that they might rate highly (Seaver, 2022, p. 59). The use of data proxies in the form of measuring interest by tracking clicks and time spent scrolling allows engineers to maximize browsing and clicking (and, ideally, sales), rather than to predict ratings.

Especially when it comes to personalization algorithms that offer recommendations, more data means more opportunities to detect relevant patterns in consumer behaviour (Bucher, 2018), and online retailers will accept dataflows from any source they can. In this 'big data' environment, where more data is seen by companies as a competitive edge, data that triangulates users' identities becomes a commodity that can be 'consumed, bought, sold, and stolen' (Cohn, 2019, p. 78) across different platforms. This is another way in which algorithms are socio-technical assemblages: it is not only the human coders that create and tinker with algorithms, but also human users who make algorithms more effective by providing them with up-to-date data. This circularity – using data generated by users to market to those same users – is essentially the basis of the online economy in which sites are free for users because they are paying for them with their own data production (Jarrett, 2022).

Although we can't know all the ways that Amazon collects data to power its bookselling algorithms, we do know of several proprietary sources. The first is Amazon's e-reading device, the Kindle. When readers use the Kindle, they produce a 'digital data trail', made up of information on pages turned, time spent reading, and pages left unread, that is uploaded to Amazon's servers (Striphas, 2010). Like other e-commerce platforms,

Amazon is able to collect data from the users who search and click through its own site, but it has vastly increased this data pool by buying several competing bookish sites: AbeBooks, launched in 1996 and bought in 2008, and Goodreads, launched in 2007 and bought in 2013. These sites, and particularly Goodreads, offer both the explicit data of ratings, reviews, and the 'tagging' of books into user-generated categories, along with the implicit data of users' clicking, scrolling, and spending time on book-pages (by which I mean not the page of a book, but the book's dedicated page on a website; the skeuomorphism here is meaningful in that time spent on the latter acts as a potential data proxy for money spent on the first). Through these purchases, Amazon has essentially cornered the market on data produced by book-buyers online, data that is produced as part of attempts to form bookish communities. As one Goodreads user said after the sale of Goodreads to Amazon: 'did it never occur to us Goodreads members that what seemed like a book-lover's paradise was actually a fantastically valuable chunk of pure data just ripe for the mining?' (quoted in Murray, 2021, p. 979). As we'll see, the mining metaphor that depicts Amazon as an extractor of a precious, natural resource will recur, high-lighting the concept that data is a 'natural' resource – a commons – pro-duced freely by users yet colonized and privatized by corporations.

The ubiquity of Amazon's data collection (see also Amazon's Alexa smart home device and Ring doorbell camera) is certainly part of what Shoshana Zuboff (2019, p. xiii), calls surveillance capitalism: 'a new economic order that claims human experience as free raw material for hidden commercial practices of extraction, prediction, and sales', but it is also what Thompson (2021) calls 'information capital'. Because of its large share of the US book market, Amazon has 'exclusive proprietary information on the browsing and purchas-ing practices of a large proportion of book buyers, far more than any retail organization ever had before' (Thompson, 2021, p. 194). It uses this mono-poly on the data market, particularly in contrast to other booksellers, to sell advertising, to compete with Google and Facebook for advertising revenue, and, most importantly for our purposes, to feed its algorithms and better target recommendations to users. Amazon's access to this data is particularly striking given that scholars (and publishers) have often lamented the lack of data surrounding reading and reception history (Squires, 2020). This data is now available, but it is owned by Amazon; scholars who want to access it must use data-scraping technologies, and are never able to access Amazon's entire data set (Walsh and Antoniak, 2021).

A Probable Reality

What algorithms do is turn this data into what companies like Amazon interpret as behavioural knowledge about their customers. Especially with books, where resale to the same customer of the same item is rare, there is necessarily an element of prediction surrounding what book a particular user will want to purchase next. In order to accomplish this, algorithms use probabilities to determine a 'best' recommendation within what is called the 'space of probable action' (Ananny, 2016, p. 107).

The earliest definition of probability theory dates from Gerolamo Cardano in 1565. Cardano's point of reference was gambling; he proposed comparing the number of casts of a die resulting in a favourable result to the number of casts resulting in unfavourable results (Smith, 2019). This is the basis of frequentist statistics, which works by repeating an event like the roll of a die and seeing how many achieve a given result. If the given result occurs 15 times out of the 100 rolls, a frequentist statistician would assume that the probability of that event occurring on the next roll is 15 per cent. What has happened in the past becomes quantified into a model for the future. This formalization of past events into future belief is the purpose of determining probabilities. As Smith (2019, p. 33) notes, the German word for probable, 'wahrscheinlich' – literally 'seeming true', does a good job of emphasizing the tension between what we know to have been true in the past (what is 'approvable'), and what we believe might be true in the future (what is 'credible'). This is the function of recommendation algorithms: to turn true historical data into a credible predictor of future conditions.

This only works if you have an event that occurs with some frequency, like a coin flip. What about an event that has never happened before? You've never bought David Mitchell's *Cloud Atlas*. Does that mean the probability of you buying it in the future is zero? On the contrary, the purchase of a book might in fact *decrease* the odds of your buying it again. In 1910, Charles Sanders Pierce addressed this problem by reframing the interpretation of probabilities not as frequencies, but as 'propensities' (Smith, 2019, p. 51), which means that you can read a statistic of some past events as a reliable indicator of the propensity of some *different* future event. The question now becomes: what sorts of past events can reliably predict a future event that has never happened? Maybe you would be more likely to purchase *Cloud Atlas* if you've already bought one of Mitchell's other novels? Other novels by authors named David? Other novels with 'Cloud' in the title? Other novels published in the same year? Other novels with the same number of pages? Other novels with similarly designed covers? Programmers sort through these possible parameters and decide which might correlate with a felicitous recommendation.

Algorithms on sites like Amazon use Bayesian statistics, named for Thomas Bayes, whose 'Essay Towards Solving a Problem in the Doctrine of Chances' was posthumously published in 1761 and laid out the foundations of modern probability theory. Unlike frequentist statistics, Bayesian statistics incorporates what are sometimes called 'subjective beliefs'. The calculation begins with a 'prior belief'. Then an experiment, such as a coin toss or a user's click on the image of a book cover, tests and updates that belief to a new, posterior belief (Smith, 2019). The original belief is predetermined by the experimenter, who might be a programmer or an algorithm. Because the resulting model of future probability is contingent on the prior belief, algorithms, like those on Amazon, are often programmed to 'believe', as their starting point, the most profitable option (Joque, 2022, p. 156). They might, for example, suggest the newest bestseller, only available in hardcover. As the clicks of users update algorithms' beliefs, the operation of these algorithms approximates something like the idea of the free market, in which the voluntary choices of buyers and sellers, or in this case algorithms and users, work together to optimize the well-being of both. Of course, the choices made by algorithms and users alike are always already constrained by algorithms' programming. As Justin Joque (2022, p. 175) writes, the use of probabilities in algorithms works to tether its outputs to reality through 'economic advantage and risk'. In this sense, algorithms 'reflect not the world as it is, but rather the world *as it is profitable*'.

This reliance on subjective beliefs might have the effect of shaking our faith in the authority of algorithmic outputs, but algorithms maintain their claim to mathematical accuracy based on their use of what is called a p-value. The p-value is a measure of how close a result or set of results is to the 'null-hypothesis' – the prior belief. If we assume that out of 100 coin flips, 50 will turn up heads, and 50 do turn up heads, we have a p-value of 0, a highly accurate probability. If we conduct the experiment and get heads ninety times, we have a high p-value, and, generally, a failed experiment.

The idea of the p-value originates in a different case of technological measurement, namely Galileo's attempts to measure the distance from Earth to a star. Although there is only one correct measurement, Galileo and others consistently arrived at disparate results. By discarding extremely large or small results, and then taking the median of the remaining numbers, Galileo achieved a result that he felt most confident was probably closest to the true number. The implication is that there are the same number of high measurements as low measurements surrounding the most accurate measurement. If graphed, these measurements would form a bell curve: many measurements would be near the correct number, a few measurements would be either too high or too low, and very few would be far off the mark. The bell curve is a natural result of human error in measuring things that are not easily observable (Smith, 2019, p. 76).

P-values – acceptable ranges for deviations from a correct measurement – are important for the functioning of contemporary algorithms. For example, in an algorithm trained to identify handwriting, it is not efficient to tell it that there are twenty-six characters it should be looking for and provide a sample of each. Instead, the algorithm is tasked with analyzing and grouping a large set of data into its own statistical categories. A given marking is grouped into a set of markings that share features within a pre-determined range of deviation (a p-value). If this algorithm creates a 27th category, this does not mean that it has discovered a 27th letter. It simply means that some marking in the dataset is different from the other twenty-six consistently enough for the algorithm to think that it is probably not one of them. This is when a human (who knows that this is not a credible result) would need to adjust the algorithm's parameters so that it reflects the world as we know it to be true (Dourish, 2016). A human might change the setting of the acceptable p-value, or she might tinker with the data, removing some of the outliers that are creating unwanted outcomes. In 1937, for example, when a test result seemed to indicate that women were slightly more intelligent than men, the test was changed to include more questions presumably easily answerable by men in order to 'correct' what was seen as an error (Smith, 2019, p. 90). Correcting what is an acceptable range of 'error' (which can only exist in relation to some predetermined, 'correct' output), influences how algorithms model our reality.

As measurements and the bell curve moved from the sciences to the social sciences, a category error was introduced. The idea of distribution around a most-measured result led to the bell curve being read as though there was a single desirable norm around which actual people and behaviours *should* fall within varying degrees of deviation. In, for example, Charles Darwin's work, the bell curve modelled genetic deviations over a population; however, when Herbert Spencer translated Darwin's work into the social sphere, he coined the term 'survival of the fittest', (a phrase only at times adopted by Darwin) which transformed the peak of the bell curve from a frequently measured observation into the measure of the ideal specimen. As Smith (2019, p. 84) notes, this transformation is important because it changes the causality of evolution; it creates the idea of objective fitness that a species must match teleologically, when, in Darwin's work, 'fitness' is simply a description of features that survive and reproduce. The idea of deviations from an a priori standard, rather than a distribution of measurements, introduced a normative and ideological angle into the observation and analysis of human behaviour.

Probabilities and statistics are a method for making order out of disorder; they are a 'machine that turns data into both value and scientific law' (Joque, 2022, p. 31). But, as Joque (2022, p. 23) notes, these outputs are not right or wrong, true or false; they are, like a commodity price at market or the value of the stock market at the closing bell, a momentary objectification and quantification of our social relations. And our faith in this objectification is a mere century or so old. Norbert Wiener (1989, pp. 10–11), writing in 1950, traces it to the rise of quantum physics: where physics used to be concerned with what will *always* happen, suddenly, physics became concerned with 'what will happen with an overwhelming probability'. This means that in a discipline that aims to observe and measure our universe, 'chance has been admitted, not merely as a mathematical tool for physics, but as part of its warp and weft'. Kate Crawford (2021, p. 213) sees the origin of a cultural emphasis on prediction and 'faith that mathematical formalisms would help us understand humans as a society', in military-funded research of signal processing and optimization during World War II. Crawford interprets this as a paradigm shift: 'the belief that accurate prediction is fundamentally about reducing the complexity of the world gave rise to an implicit theory of the social: find the signal in the noise and make order from disorder'. In short, the idea that probabilities can accurately quantify and predict human behaviour is historically contingent.

So although, as Smith (2019, p. 85) says, what is needed is probability literacy – an understanding of 'the difference between algorithms' quantitative view of the world and the real-world reality of how people interact and co-operate in real populations' – this would require 'overcoming a long-cherished utopian belief that populations will inevitably optimize and that people and their behaviour can be reduced to simplistic, quantifiable features'. A faith in algorithmic outputs is a faith in the reducibility of human interaction and their eventual optimization, especially at the level of the population.

This type of literacy is made increasingly difficult by the computing power of algorithms, which allows them to conduct calculations in fractions of seconds. In 2008, Chris Anderson wrote that the amount of data and computing power available would change our epistemological attitude toward the world. We would no longer need to build simplified models and test them against the complexities of the real world; the complexities of the world could, instead, just be computed in real time. He called this the 'End of Theory'. Although models help us understand the world, Anderson (2008a) argued, with algorithms, understanding becomes overrated: 'who knows why people do what they do? The point is they do it, and we can track and measure it with unprecedented fidelity. With enough data, the numbers speak for themselves'. Like another of Borges's stories, where cartographers make a map that corresponds exactly to the size of an empire, technology here is used not to help model and understand but as a replacement – a simulacrum – of reality. As I've tried to show here, this view ignores the fact that statistics is a heuristic, historically rooted in a desire to predict the future using whatever data from the past is available.

It is not, as Smith (2019, p. 62) reminds us, 'some magic formula that can predict the future'. Rather, it is a quantification of the future within adjustable ranges of deviation using available data proxies, all veiled by the power of rapid computation: a mystification of our own behaviours.

It is worth saying here that the concept of probability is a technology, and we should therefore be wary of deterministic accounts of its use. We might suggest that a human bookseller who gives you a recommendation is 'running an internal model of [her] own' (O'Neil, 2016, p. 209) when she recommends *Parable of the Sower* after learning that you are a fan of Nnedi Okorafor. And although the bookseller's mind similarly appears as a black box (this is the conceit of psychoanalysis), the difference is that we can ask the bookseller *why* she provides a particular recommendation. Of course, she might dissemble. She says *Parable of the Sower* is a classic work of speculative fiction by another Black woman author that she has enjoyed reading several times, but she has actually ordered too many copies and needs to turn over her stock. But this is the risk of all social interactions – they are acts of faith. Algorithmic recommendations are acts of faith in a more fundamental way: they refuse the question of *why*. They use, as James Bridle (2018, p. 147) writes, 'statistical inference [...] to remove understanding from the equation and replace it with data-driven correlation'.

Machine Learning and Algorithmic Subjects

Imagine now that you are a programmer who is trying to figure out what types of data will help you determine whether a user will click on a recommended book. Some factors to consider might be the genre of the book, how recently it has been published, and its user ratings. But how much weight should you give to each factor? With machine learning, algorithms respond to data inputs (like a click or no click) by reweighting the inputs autonomously. After being programmed with a particular goal – achieve a click on the first page of search results or achieve a click on a recommendation 5 per cent of the time – algorithms will adjust their own code to revise the mixture of inputs to achieve this goal. This saves time and labour because algorithms can incorporate new data and reweight inputs much more quickly than a human (nearly instantaneously).

These programmed aims have shifted along with the increased importance of data proxies. Whereas the aim was once to make more accurate predictions of what users would *like*, the aim now is often to make predictions that will encourage users to spend more time on the site, clicking, scrolling, and producing more data. Like the role of the bookstore cafe, intended primarily to get traffic in the door, these algorithms aim to increase interaction with the site. Certainly, if users spend more time on a site, they are more likely to make a purchase, but this aim is secondary to the aim of harvesting more freely produced data. This is what Seaver (2022, p. 58) calls 'captivation metrics', which successful algorithms aim to improve.

A human-controlled example of machine learning is A/B testing. When you're browsing the internet, it is likely that the results of a search or the appearance of various pages is not the same for all other users. A/B tests present different versions (sometimes up to five or ten) of a page to different audiences to assess permutations of algorithms. After enough data is collected (over the course of hours or several months), the programmers will know which version was more successful at achieving the desired results. Users usually aren't aware that they are part of this experiment, nor that the site they are seeing is not the same site that other users are seeing (Bucher, 2018). Importantly, this means that it is difficult to ever talk about *the* algorithm as though it is one thing. Rather, algorithms are '"permanently beta", always changing and never solidifying into a final form' (Seaver, 2022, p. 60). They are often multiple, and, using machine learning, always evolving with users' behaviours in real time.

Machine learning brings into question our position in relation to algorithms. As one of the founders of OKCupid once said: 'Guess what, everybody: if you use the Internet, you're the subject of hundreds of experiments at any given time, on every site. That's how websites work' (quoted in O'Shea, 2019, p. 31). If, at first, we felt we were the autonomous subjects that algorithms aimed to reflect, we are now its test subjects, which is to say the *objects* of its experiment. The slippage is inherent in the word *subject* itself, which we use to describe people as conscious and thinking beings as well as objects of external authority, and captures something of the recursivity of machine learning in which the calculations of people and the calculations of algorithms cooperatively and iteratively shape the virtual environment (Gillespie, 2014). Humans shape future algorithmic outputs by choosing some outputs over others, but algorithms shape human practices by offering targeted choices and avenues to interact with its outputs. While we are reading algorithmic outputs, algorithms are reading us and our reactions to them.

Algorithms' views of us are limited by the actions we take online, but in shaping these actions, algorithms also intervene in shaping our online selves, which are as John Cheney-Lippold (2017, p. 31) writes 'utterly overdetermined'. When we interact with algorithms, we can confirm their view of us or surprise them by refuting their prior beliefs about what we will do. In either case we are conforming to the options presented and expected by them. For algorithms, as Florian Cramer (2018, p. 27) writes, 'the reduction of audience members to countable numbers – data sets, indices – is [...] a self-fulfilling prophecy of stability'. These datafied versions of ourselves, as Joque (2022, pp. 180–182) writes, are made of up 'interchangeable bits' that render 'the previously incommensurate', what we might call our unique subjectivity, 'as commensurate, thus rendering it understandable'. In this sense, our online selves – the selves that confront algorithms and are recommended products by them – are algorithmically processed and produced in ways that are easily understood, compared, and communicated back to us.

Let's return to Sumpter's (2018, p. 106) comparison of the way algorithms know you to the way a work of literature can create a sense of personalized experience or social connection. Like algorithms, literature relies on the input of a human reader to make meaning, and it is undeniable that the best novels not only hail a reader, but also discipline that reader in the norms of meaning-making constructed by the novel. The self reading the novel is arguably shaped by the novel, just as the novel is at mercy of the reader to read generously, openly, carefully, etc. Of course this is not machine learning. Putting aside 'choose your own adventure' books and digital novels with multiple possible hyperlinked pathways, traditional novels cannot really change in response to the reader's interpretation. Every reader, we might say, reads the same page, although no two readers really read the same novel. This is because there is something incommensurate about our subjectivity, something that is not equivalent when two humans read the same text.

When Sumpter equates the hailing of algorithms with the hailing of the novel ('Sometimes when I am deep in a good novel, I believe that no other person will ever talk to me in the way this writer has talked to me. A few hours on Amazon dispels this illusion entirely'.) the 'me' he is talking about is a changing designation. A text hails a thinking subject, offering it the opportunity to collaboratively make meaning; algorithms hail a digital dossier, offering it the opportunity to confirm or deny a statistically derived image of an algorithmically produced self.

In many ways, recommendation algorithms and human booksellers share similar aims: to match readers and books, to increase traffic, and to 'capture' book buyers. They may even consider many of the same factors in concluding what books to feature or recommend. A major distinction, due to algorithmic quantification of human behaviour, is the speed and automaticity of algorithms' results. This is, however, a nontrivial difference. Speed, or rather its absence, is central to our cultural understanding of what a book and, as Jessica Pressman (2020) puts it, 'bookishness' is. Reading a book, compared to a downloading a file, is 'a slow form of exchange'. Pressman (p. 58) quotes Christina Lupton as saying that 'there's a slowing down, a repetition, a promise, associated with book reading that pulls back on the logic of accumulation and acceleration, and the measurement of time'. The logic of accumulation and acceleration, though, is key to Amazon's 'epic narrative', in which its 'great, quasi-imperial sprawl' and 'seemingly unbounded ambition to multi-national if not multiplanetary commercial presence' (McGurl, 2021b, p. 394) keeps an eventual narrative dénouement at bay. In fact, slowing down is the number one threat to Amazon's hegemony of the book world. As Kate Crawford (2021, p. 230) records: 'Bezos is worried. His fear is that the planet's growing energy demands will soon outstrip its limited supply. For him, the greatest concern "is not necessarily extinction" but *stasis*: "We will have to stop growing, which I think is a very bad future"'.

As we move to the next section, in which we explore Amazon's search and recommendation algorithms, we'll find again that speed – of search, recommendation, and delivery – is the logic valorized by Amazon. When contrasted with the slowing down of the brick-and-mortar bookstore, associated with words like 'browsing' – a word whose meaning picks up on the sense of grazing or nourishing the self over an extended period of time – we'll see that speed is not just incidental to algorithms, it is their fundamental affordance and it shapes our relationship to books, bookstores, and the humans who populate them.

3 Searching for and Recommending Books

The fact that Amazon can offer nearly every in-print book in English is both its competitive advantage and an immense challenge if the goal of the bookstore is uniting each reader with the 'right' book. No brick-and-mortar bookstore, as Ann Steiner (2017, p. 19) writes, can offer every available book; 'rather', she says, 'it is in its selection that each bookshop is unique'. Bookstores mediate between publishers and consumers, predetermining the selection that buyers will see. It is this cultural work that many see as the primary value of the bookstore (Miller, 2006). Mark Forsyth (2014), in his paean for the bookstore called *The Unknown Unknown: Bookshops and the Delight of Not Getting What You Wanted*, privileges the traditional bookstore's spontaneous discoveries by contrasting a well-curated selection of books with a Borgesian universal library: 'If a bookshop contained every book ever written, what are the chances that you would find the *one* book you need? . . . . No, the perfect bookshop is small, small and selective. You should be able to go in blindfolded, reach out your hand at random and find something wonderful'.

The small and selective bookshop might stock only 'wonderful' things, but 'wonderful' to whom? This is the argument of Anderson (2008b), who uses the term 'the long tail' to describe the vast majority of books (or songs or movies) that aren't bestsellers or haven't been recently published (see Figure 2). These items, although they are likely to have some audience, are not likely to be stocked in most brick-and-mortar stores because their audiences are too small (think a few downloads or sales a month across a national population). The seemingly unlimited stock of online stores like Amazon now makes the long tail accessible to consumers. (Customers have always had access to this long tail by requesting that a bookseller order a book they don't have in stock; however, this service was not well-advertised, and it remains more inconvenient than having a book delivered straight to your door without leaving the house (Miller, 2013)). Anderson (2008b, p. 10) argues that connecting these niche audiences with works in the long tail uncovers a significant market that has been there, untapped all along: 'the invisible market', he says, 'has turned visible'. No longer limited by a physical footprint, or a local

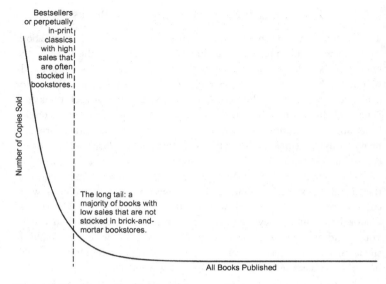

Figure 2 The long tail of book sales.

audience, online retailers can sell everything to everyone, or perhaps it's anything to anyone, matching specific users with specific, at times arcane or esoteric products. While Amazon's top 100,000 books do sell reliably (98 per cent sell at least once a quarter), more than a quarter of Amazon's book sales come from outside of the top 100,000 (Anderson, 2008b, pp. 8–9). This benefits publishers, who agree that sales from their backlist (books published a year or more ago) have increased since being listed on Amazon. For one publisher, 90 per cent of sales from the deep backlist are made on Amazon, and it has been estimated that about 75 per cent of Amazon's book sales are from the backlist (Bury and Kean, 2005).

Imagine walking through a bookstore that is a million square feet (the size of an average Amazon fulfilment centre, although one in Tennessee takes up 3.6 million square feet). What are the chances that your eye will happen to land on the book you were looking for, or perhaps the book you didn't know you were looking for? In the past, a bookstore's stock, or even the bookseller herself would act as a search or recommendation engine, narrowing down possible options; on Amazon, algorithms take over this function, making some books visible while keeping others hidden. Here's Bezos (quoted in Pariser, 2012, p. 25), who waxes nostalgic on the function of the bookseller that he aims to replace with algorithms, paradoxically wanting to go 'back to the days of the small bookseller who got to know you very well and would say things like, "I know you like John Irving, and guess what, here's this one author, I think he's a lot like John Irving"'. Replicating this sort of personalization at an enormous scale is the aim of Amazon's search and recommendation algorithms.

Whereas Forsyth would like to enter a bookstore, close his eyes and stumble across a good book, engineers like Yunkai Zhai and Wei Lu (2017) present algorithms as eye-opening, keeping consumers from going 'blindly ... to various places to find their own books'. But Thompson (2021, p. 190) doubts that algorithms really provide this sort of clear-eyed access to a universal library. He suggests that algorithms act as a sort of pen light in an immense darkness: 'you switch on the pen light and you can see only what's immediately in front of you, while the millions of other books that fill this vast library are plunged into darkness'. 'The reality', Thompson suggests, 'is worse than the metaphor because in the real world of algorithm-driven recommendations, it is Amazon, not you, that controls the pen light, decides when to turn it on and where to point it and when to turn it off again'. So, how do these algorithms decide where to point the pen light? This is the question that propels this section.

Item-to-Item Filtering

When algorithmic outputs tell you that a book is like a book by John Irving, it is conducting item-to-item filtering. It models all the books in its inventory, using the data to make statistical groupings of ones that are alike. So far, so similar to what a human bookseller might do. But we might expect a bookseller to have read at least some of the books they are grouping together. Although there are algorithms that 'read' texts, used by researchers interested in asking questions about word frequency or language modelling, most item-to-item filtering on bookselling sites does not base its account of books' similarities on what we would consider their content. Rather, a book's content for item-to-item filtering algorithms is made up of data proxies and might include things like its title, summary, outline, author, year of publication, publication, genre, and number of pages (Alharthi, Inkpen, and Szpakowicz, 2018).

These algorithms are reading not books but book metadata. Imagine, for the sake of relative simplicity, a graph in three dimensions where each dimension represents a data input: author, year of publication, and genre. Each book becomes a point in this space, but the groupings of points (i.e. what authors are most similar to one another, or what genres are most 'like' other genres) are distributed by a statistical model deployed by algorithms, which uses human inputs (datafied preferences for different authors, years of publication, and genres) to adjust the weight of each factor. Perhaps the year of publication is trivial in determining what books are alike, but authorship is very important. This is how algorithms tell you that you might like an author who is 'like' John Irving: the 'likeness' is statistically determined by comparing the relevant metadata of a book with that of another book (sort of like the handwriting algorithm from the last section that sorted 'like' markings into different categories). Now imagine this space in ten or twenty dimensions. This is only possible for us in the most abstract of senses, which is precisely the point of algorithmic computing power.

Recommendations for books that are similar to the book whose page you are looking at (the 'focal product') are called cross-recommendations, and their function is often not to encourage a click on the recommended book (although they might), but rather to sell the focal product (Zhu, Wang, and Chang, 2018). If you are contemplating buying a book and see felicitous cross-recommendations (perhaps of books you've already read and enjoyed) then you'll be more likely to buy the book in question. But this process has misfired in the past. Brad Stone (2013, p. 114), Bezos's biographer, tells the story of the product page for *The Subtle Knife*, the sequel to the young adult novel *The Golden Compass*. The cross-recommendations generated by algorithms were of switchblades and SS weaponry kits, which created tension between the Amazon editors responsible for the book department and Joel Spiegel, Vice President of Engineering, who is quoted as saying that 'the person whose mission in life was to sell children's books would storm into [his] office yelling, why the hell do I have Nazi memorabilia listed on my page?' Cross-recommendations have a politics, and it is a politics that algorithms cannot comprehend nor, according to the corporations that deploy them, be held responsible for. This output was not generated by mistake. The algorithms were working as intended, reproducing the strong correlation that exists between the word *Knife* in the title of the novel and the metadata of the objects up for sale. But, as any human understands, this recommendation is not felicitous. In fact we might consider it ethically egregious.

Because item-to-item filtering relies on metadata, it is subject to traditional critiques of hierarchical organization systems in that the categories used to define the data are rooted in Eurocentric ontologies of what a book is and what meaningfully distinguishes it from other books. Alexandra Dane (2023) writes that Amazon categorizes romance novels by white authors as 'romance fiction' and romance novels by Black authors as 'Black romance fiction'. When these categories are input into algorithms, 'whiteness', as Dane (2023, p. 27) writes, 'as a generic or primary category of classification not only influences perceptions around subjects and people but also feeds into mechanisms by which books are sold and circulated . . . when readers are searching for romance fiction on Amazon, they will primarily see the titles by White authors and the titles by Black authors will only surface if they are specifically searched for'. Here, the pen light is deliberately turned towards white authors, only making books by Black authors visible if a user knows that they are accessible through different search terms. This act of segregation through metadata becomes a formal constraint on the possibilities available to users as they navigate their interaction with Amazon's algorithms.

Although book metadata is often entered by the publishers wishing to list their books on the site, Amazon's algorithms may also use metadata generated by users on its affiliate sites. For example, Melanie Walsh and Maria Antoniak (2021, p. 248) point to Goodreads, where users metaphorically shelve books in their libraries in order to tag them. These 'collaborative tagging systems produce "folk taxonomies" or folksonomies, classification systems built by communities from the ground up'. When Amazon's algorithms incorporate user tags as part of their item-to-item filtering, they reflect not only the categories of publishers, but also the categories most useful to users, whose behaviours are, after all, the ones algorithms are attempting to mirror, reinforce, and redirect. But even the democratically produced folksonomies on Goodreads are not necessarily more diverse than those generated by publishers. Walsh and Antoniak (2021, p. 254) note that 94 per cent of books tagged as 'classics' by Goodreads users are by white authors, which makes this folksonomic canon of classics whiter than either the canon of authors recommended by the Advanced Placement program (a college-credit program available in some US high schools) (70 per cent) or the canon of books created by syllabi available on Open Syllabus (80 per cent).

Categorizing books, even without algorithms, is a fraught endeavour, always reflecting the historical and cultural perspectives of the categorizer. Whether books by women are more likely to be categorized as young adult, or whether books by Black authors are more likely to be grouped in categories like 'Black writing' rather than the genre they participate in, categorization implicates publishers' marketing campaigns, bookstore and library shelving schemes, and audiences alike. Algorithms and the metadata they rely on aren't the root of this issue; however, when algorithms use these categories to compute recommendations rapidly and repeatedly, they entrench them, presenting affiliations between categories as natural and perhaps even causal. Are works by Black romance authors really all more alike to each other than they are to any works by White romance authors? If we accept algorithmic recommendations as a mirror of reality rooted in data, then we might be led to think so.

When we accept a cross-recommendation or acknowledge its felicity, we are accepting the organizational logic that made it possible, without being able to question it. Brick-and-mortar bookstores, of course, have their own organization systems, usually by occasionally esoteric subjects or genres, then alphabetically by author. The difference is that these logics are exposed and laid bare to the critique of every customer who enters the store. How can we critique a logic that, on the one hand we are deeply implicated in, and yet, on the other hand, remains so difficult to track, updating itself in real-time?

Personalization and Serendipity

Algorithms can entrench problematic ontologies when they filter books by race or gender, but because item-to-item filtering uses metadata that isn't readily visible to customers browsing a traditional bookstore, it can also make visible books that might have remained invisible otherwise. Iris van der Tuin (2023, pp. 190–195) corrects a too technologically deterministic view of algorithmic filtering through her autobiographical narration of a serendipitous discovery she made on Google Books – E. L. Young's *Philosophy of Reality*, published in 1930. The book appeared in response to one of her queries unrelated to E. L. Young, and van der Tuin says that she would have ignored the book in a bookstore. 'I was not looking for a book of metaphysics', she writes, 'as a scholar, I am not primarily interested in contributing to research about or in researching with male philosophers'. However, the Google Books metadata that enabled this search algorithm told her that E. L. Young was really Eva Louise Young, which began van der Tuin's work of recovering the biography of the British philosopher. 'I really needed Google Books to "gender" E. L. Young', van der Tuin writes. In this example, metadata makes the invisible (E. L. Young's small oeuvre and gender) visible to the right reader, which is the idea behind accessing the ever-growing long tail of books.

The key is to finding the right reader, which is accomplished through personalization. This means that Amazon's algorithms will consider what they know about you – the *you* they have pieced together from your clicks, scrolls, and views – when generating outputs. Although everything on Amazon's site might be technically available to everyone, not everyone sees the same outputs, which are customized to 'fit your known locality, interests, obsessions, fetishes, and points of view' at least in so far as they have been captured by data proxies. This is called 'narrowcasting', and it is very efficient if you are looking for something that is consistent with the types of things you have looked for in the past. However, as Siva Vaidhyanathan (2011, p. 183) writes, narrowcasting means that 'you are less likely to stumble on the unexpected, the unknown, the unfamiliar, and the uncomfortable'. In van der Tuin's case, the search result became felicitous precisely because algorithms seem to have anticipated her existing interest in female philosophers.

Of course, when we enter a search term and search algorithms return results influenced by our search histories, location, and other data points, we are not required to accept the first result, or even the second or third, and we can usually re-sort results according to various logics ('most relevant' or 'newest first'). Yet, we are being guided 'toward certain choices over others in order to encourage [us] to better fit in with those the system recognizes as being like [us]'. As Cohn (2019, p. 7) writes, algorithms can be disciplining in that they 'present consumer desires, preferences, and tastes as key to divining who you are, where you fit in, and how to become the best you that you can be'. In other words, a list of search results tailored to us gives us not only a narrow view of what exists in the world but also might influence our view of ourselves. If the results on the first page are not felicitous, does that mean that the algorithms are broken? That you don't really know what you're looking for? That you're looking for the wrong thing? If viewed naively, we might understand our personalized search results as saying more about us than about the logics underlying the organization of the metadata.

Much has been made of the fact that through personalization, algorithms allow marketers to stop relying on racialized and gendered demographic data because ads can be targeted directly to individuals. But this is only partially true. Although race is usually not something that algorithms 'know' about you, they do model it, and sites like Amazon sell advertising based on the race of users. Goodreads users are, for example, listed as '77% Caucasian, 9% Hispanic, 7% African American, 6% Asian, and 1% other' (Walsh and Antoniak, 2021, p. 255). These figures aren't self-reported. They are statistically modelled by a company called Quantcast, which uses these algorithmically produced demographic groups to sell advertising on the site. These labels don't refer to how we (unevenly) experience race in the real world. When algorithms statistically model a user's data profile as belonging to a racial group it means that this user clicks and buys, within a set amount of deviation, *like* other members of that group. If their clicking and buying patterns change, they might be grouped with and labelled as a different race. Furthermore, the racialized labels are not used or understood by algorithms, but are added by humans who require them in order to interpret (and monetize) the groupings created through statistical modelling (Seaver, 2022, p. 125).

The groups created when search algorithms show some users particular results and others different results are often called silos or filter bubbles. Whereas a bookstore's window display (which, as Steiner (2015) notes, is carefully curated and never random) is intended to entice as many passersby as possible, Amazon's pages are made just for you, reflecting your interests insofar as algorithms know what they are. This is often what makes the recommendations feel so felicitous, gratifying, or, as Sumpter writes, like algorithms understand you. Joseph Turow (quoted in O'Shea, 2019, p. 26) sees this, somewhat like Bezos does, as a return to a more personal shopping experience, this time like a peddler who travels door to door making assumptions about what you might want to buy and how much to charge you based on the appearance of your home and previous visits. And although this sort of empathetic social connection might seem appealing, tailored transactions mean that people of different races, genders, and income brackets see a different internet and a different bookstore (O'Shea, 2019). The existence of filter bubbles has been difficult for researchers to prove, and, as Seaver (2022) notes, responses to its existence are often theoretical: the real filter bubble is the small town without access to the internet (or a bookstore), and algorithms expand those bubbles rather than shrink them. But if we see Amazon's algorithms, as Striphas (2023, p. 14) does, as 'perform[ing] curatorial work comparable to that of a museum' then acknowledging that we're all in a different bookstore means that we all have access to different understandings of both the past of literary production and our opportunities for reading in the future.

Of course we might say that independent bookstores create the same segmentation of audiences, revealing different books to different local (and socio-economic) audiences, and that, in fact, the appeal of search or recommendation algorithms is that they are bypassing this sort of human gatekeeping. Readers and publishers are no longer at the whim of a stuffy, old bookseller who gets to decide what is legitimate or important and what isn't. Jenni Ramone (2020, p. 87) provides an example of small Nigerian presses like Cassava Republic and Paressia, who, through online marketplaces like Amazon, 'are able to compete with global publishers online, meaning that alongside the celebrated migrant Nigerian authors writing for a global audience, more 'locally' inflected Nigerian literary texts are finding a route to a broader literary market'. These presses don't have to convince US bookstores to stock their books; they can just offer books on Amazon and, as part of the long tail of book production, find their audience from within a large pool of global readers. In this way, algorithms work as Anderson had hoped, producing more democratic access to books and undercutting hierarchies in bookselling. This is particularly useful for global readers who are already interested in work from small presses in Nigeria. There is, however, no way of knowing how often algorithms are recommending these books over others. These presses are still at the whim of a mediator, just one they do not have to (nor are able to) appeal to.

The data used by algorithms like Amazon's comes primarily from users in North America and Europe, which means it is these users who influence the creation of the statistical categories that inform item-to-item filtering. Amazon and other US tech companies have been aggressively trying to access other data pools, for example in India and China, knowing that this data would allow them to appeal to a much broader global audience through what Evan Elkins (2019, p. 386) calls 'engineered cosmopolitanism'. This practice, which has put pressure on local competitors, is called 'data colonization' or 'platform imperialism' by its detractors, who see it as a way for 'US American digital platforms to accumulate power and capital by serving as the world's major conduits for communication and media practice'. Likely because of this data imbalance, studies (See Kaiser and Rauchfleisch, 2020) show that recommendation algorithms on sites like YouTube often privilege US content rather than local content even in non-Anglophone contexts.

This is not to say that brick-and-mortar bookstores are more diverse than online bookselling, and, as Caroline Koegler and Corinna Norrick-Rühl write, the gatekeepers of contemporary fiction in the brick-and-mortar world are still 'disproportionately white, male, cisgendered, heterosexual, and able-bodied' (75) and we should be suspicious of claims that protecting bookstores through, for example, fixed pricing laws, automatically protects 'diversity' (15–16). However, we should also remain sceptical that algorithms produce this diversity, and, if they do so, that they do so evenly for all users. After all, algorithms are designed to please us, and, from the perspective of algorithms, there's no guarantee that diversifying what they shine their pen light on will do so.

The examples of small Nigerian publishers and van der Tuin's discovery of E. L. Young show how search algorithms don't always create silos and can in fact change our future in positive ways by cataloguing and retrieving the past and present. However, there is a synchronic logic of algorithmic categorization that might thwart or be slow to detect and reflect positive changes that happen in reality (Seaver, 2022). Because algorithms accrue data over time, historical data amasses, and new data becomes an ever-shrinking percentage of the input used to make a recommendation or return a search result. Another way of thinking about this is that if millions of clicks have reinforced a 'prior belief', a new experiment will do little to move the needle. Ed Finn (2012), for example, shows that historical syllabi data is embedded in Amazon's cross-recommendations on product pages of frequently assigned books and that these affiliations may be very slow to change (see Figures 3 and 4). Algorithms are programmed not to take risks by suggesting results that

Figure 3 The book page of *1984* by George Orwell features cross-recommendations for Jane Austen's *Pride and Prejudice*, Fyodor Dostoyevsky's *Crime and Punishment*, and F. Scott Fitzgerald's *The Great Gatsby*.

Figure 4 The book page of *The Great Gatsby*, in turn, features cross-recommendations for Ernest Hemingway's *The Old Man and the Sea*, Arthur Miller's *The Crucible*, Shakespeare's *Othello* and *Romeo and Juliet*, and Nathaniel Hawthorne's *The Scarlet Letter*.

might surprise users, but this means they aren't programmed to anticipate our development as readers and people. As Bucher (2018, p. 104) records one YouTube user saying, algorithms 'are just based on trends and past behaviour. It can't predict for you in the future, it just assumes you are going to repeat everything you've done in the past'. Although algorithms use probabilities to predict the future, those predictions are based only on past data, not the foundational assumption that people change. While algorithms undoubtedly shape our future by shining the pen light on what we should read next, they operate as though the future doesn't exist, or at least that it will fit neatly into the same categories (within a range of deviation) that it always has in the past.

Collaborative Filtering

What I've been describing is item-to-item filtering – the creation of statistical groups of 'like' books through metadata categories. I want to now turn to collaborative filtering, which produces statistical groups of 'like' users, like the example of Quantcast's racial groups above. Whereas item-to-item filtering produces recommendations like 'Products related to this item', collaborative filtering recommendations are flagged by phrases like 'Frequently bought together'. As the prior section shows, these two types of filtering are not easily teased apart, and Amazon's algorithms likely make use of both types of filtering at once.

Like filtering that groups items together, collaborative filtering makes statistical groups of users out of their data to find those that behave most similarly. Here, clusters of points represent similar users rather than similar books. Here's how Bezos describes it:

> [collaborative filtering] is a statistical technique that looks at your past purchase stream and finds other people whose past purchase streams are similar. Think of the people it finds as your electronic soul mates. Then we look at that aggregation and see what things your electronic soul mates have bought that you haven't. Those are the books we recommend. And it works. (Sheff, 2000)

The logic is that if someone has bought some of the same books you have, you will also be interested in their most recent book purchase, which collaborative filtering algorithms will generate for you as a recommendation. Because the 'likeness' of users to other users is determined by user behaviour like clicks and scrolls, there is a sense for some observers that collaborative filtering algorithms 'facilitate interpersonal communication between customers' (Knotzer, 2008) because users become implicitly aware of the choices of other users through the recommendations.

The recommendations that appear through collaborative filtering act like Adam Smith's invisible hand: both are produced by a population of self-interested individuals whose actions manipulate what is sold and bought. Just as proponents of the free market believe that the invisible hand promotes, as Smith (2019, p. 192) writes, 'the emergence of a correct sequence of events and categorization of things that give the socially best possible arrangements of goods/prices, resulting in a desired state of equilibrium without any deliberate thinking, planning, or social policy' the idea that algorithms reflect democratic outputs privileges the idea of individual agency where it may not exist. A book that receives a lot of clicks (is 'most viewed') is not necessarily one that the majority of readers think is a good book. Books that produce more clicks are recommended to more users, making it appear as though the crowd's selection is confirming the appeal of this particular book. Really, what is being measured is algorithms' ability to induce clicking and discipline user behaviour through recommendations.

Critics like Simone Murray (2018, p. 57) worry that critiquing 'the effect of algorithmic culture on perpetuating mass-cultural trends' risks repeating a reactionary logic of elitist criticism. In order for that to be true, we would have to accept that algorithms do in fact reflect the desire of something we could call a public (Christin, 2022). This is an assumption we should scrutinize. Just as the metaphor of the invisible hand is, as Alexander Galloway (2021, p. 167) writes, 'a symptom of [Smith's] inability to correlate small-scale behavior with large-scale results' so too do algorithms occlude the complex and non-uniform relationships between an individual's click (or purchase or preference) and the shared statistical recommendation. To believe that this recommendation reflects the desires of a public, is, first, to treat, like algorithms, as commensurate each click as a positive endorsement of a book (when it may be, for example, simply a misfire or part of a sequence of browsing); second, to confuse the simplification of quantified data profiles with the desires of real people (do these soulmates actually have souls?); and, third, to ignore the over-determination of these desires by algorithms' recommendations.

Economists that aim to measure and predict the 'invisible hand' operate on nontrivial assumptions about people: 'that they are certain about everything in the world around them, stable in their perception of utility (preferences), logically rational with regard to the actions they take in their trades, and always pursuing gain for themselves relative to their preferences' (Smith, 2019, p. 190). And so, too, do collaborative filtering algorithms make assumptions about users to fit them into predetermined categories. 'Efficient and scalable systems', Mike Anannay writes, 'require stable categories of people who have learned to say certain words, click certain sequences, and move in predictable ways' (Ananny, 2016, pp. 103–104). Trying to fit algorithms' perceptions of us is what Cohn (2019, p. 158) calls the 'algorithmic gaze', 'which 'teaches us to see ourselves as if algorithmically generated and modular by design'. The algorithmic gaze is enforced by algorithms' hailing of users. Picking up on Louis Althusser's concept of the ideological state apparatus which manifests itself when a subject responds to being hailed by, for example, a police officer on the street, Cheney-Lippold (2017, p. 91) suggests that when we recognize ourselves as the 'you' of 'users like you also bought' – when we treat this recommendation as felicitous – we become interpellated into algorithms' category-based profiling. In this way, algorithms don't reflect existing publics and their desires—they shape them. As these publics become disciplined by algorithmic categories, algorithms become more and more accurate in predicting what users will do and how they will act. Just as information about the status of a particular company on the stock market isn't powerful because it's right, but because it is treated by observers as though it is right (Lamdan, 2022), so, too, do algorithms become powerful when they are read as cultural arbiters and therefore shape the behaviour that they seek to measure.

So collaborative filtering algorithms offer the best of both worlds: a computational objectivity and a perfect intersubjectivity. Or at least that's how they may be perceived. Audrey Laing and Jo Royle (2013, p. 121) record a user looking for a specific book on Amazon: 'and then there was, you know they have these things "oh people who bought your book bought also this and this" … and somehow it caught my eye and I ordered that one book and that's it, I'm an addict now!' The pen light focused on a particular book, but also positioned that book rhetorically as appealing to similar readers. Yi-Fen Chen (2008) even suggests that consumers are more interested in books labelled 'customers who bought this book also bought…' than in books recommended by bookstore staff. This is, I would suggest, because a recommendation from a single reader elicits the sense of pure subjectivity, which risks the exclusionary habits of gatekeeping, while a collection of statistically computed preferences hedges against any one voice influencing our selections. Paradoxically, algorithms make intersubjectivity appear neutral, or 'objective'; it objectifies our subjectivity.

This is why the data produced and processed by algorithms is attractive to sociologists, who see it as unearthing truths through computation. But Gillespie (2014, p. 190) warns against uncritical acceptance of algorithmic understandings of ourselves, because algorithms 'produce hieroglyphs: shaped by the tool by which they are carved, requiring of priestly interpretation, they tell powerful but often mythological stories – usually in the service of the gods'. Algorithmic interpretations of ourselves are necessarily opaque. We use them because they are able to find correlations within data at speeds beyond our human abilities, but there is no guarantee that these correlations will 'accord with human semantic explanations' (Burrell, 2016, p. 10). Algorithms might make models and language superfluous, but models and language are how we conceptualize the world and our relationships to each other. Consider Sumpter's (2018, p. 40) defence of Facebook's categorization of users using seemingly nonsense categories like 'toast' and 'platypus': 'it is important to remember that [these categories] are an attempt to put words to a much deeper algorithmic understanding that Facebook has created of its users . . . . In fact, these relationships . . . can't really be explained in words at all. We simply can't get to grips with the high-dimensional understanding Facebook has created of us'. If we can't comprehend, assess, or describe this understanding, one wonders then what use it is besides being used to sell things. But precisely because what we're interested in here is books, it seems problematic that algorithms' understanding of us when it recommends books resists elucidation in language. What we seek from books is, like the imperfect librarians of Borges's library, a catalogue of the world and of ourselves; when algorithms offer us a recommendation, they claim to offer us a version of that catalogue, while keeping any knowledge of ourselves that they have hidden in streams of data and computation.

Understanding our relationship to others through computation, as Joque (2022, p. 202) suggests, alienates us from ourselves. 'One cannot know, and thus politically act', he writes, 'if the subject has an inadequate understanding of both the terrain on which they stand and the nonlinear consequences of their actions'. The translation of human action into data is a kind of 'sorcery', making relationships 'impenetrable, taking on an impact, a power of adhesion and repulsion which makes [data] resemble their extreme antithesis, spells' (Horkheimer and Adorno, 2002, pp. 133–134). Ultimately, I want to suggest that to prefer the hailing of book recommendation algorithms to a human recommendation is to prefer a mystified understanding of ourselves – one that makes the intersubjective politics of living and reading in this world together untraceable.

It would be reasonable here to say that sure, maybe algorithms don't offer us a clear-eyed view of ourselves, but neither does an independent bookstore, which reflects only the proclivities of a shopkeeper and her own understanding of her customers. Worse, she's probably accepting marketing dollars from publishers to stock books in highly visible spaces. These dollars, called coop or cooperative advertising dollars, are funds paid by publishers to retailers to advertise and promote specific books (Miller, 2006). In a brick-and-mortar store, the funds usually buy highly visible placement within the store, such as front-of-store or window display space. It's not clear to what extent customers in a brick-and-mortar store know about the existence of coop, and, therefore, that the huge stacks at the front of the store don't necessarily reflect the bookseller's book preferences. However, when Doreen Carvajal (1999) broke the story in the *New York Times* that Amazon was accepting coop dollars, customers were outraged. Carvajal reported that for $10,000 a publisher could get a book displayed on Amazon's home page or on one of the 'What We're Reading' lists. In response, Amazon refunded customers who had bought books that were funded with coop money and added 'Sponsored' tags to search and recommendation results that appeared because of publisher funding. This means that the influence of marketing dollars has become *more* transparent on Amazon than it is in brick-and-mortar bookstores.

However, when Amazon weights its algorithms to prefer books from particular publishers, these manipulations have feedback effects that will continue to show up in user data and recommendation outputs even if the coop funding stops. Unlike placement in a brick-and-mortar store, which is the same for all customers, placement on Amazon can mean targeting specific types of buyers (Thompson, 2021). If algorithms are made to appear personalized, then using coop to affect the results is a kind of 'corrupt personalization' (Cohn, 2019, p. 19). In fact, Amazon openly leverages the function of its algorithms to attract coop fees (Packer, 2014). If a publisher refuses to pay the fees, Amazon manipulates its algorithms to stop recommending books by a particular publisher, which can cause sales to drop by as much as 40 per cent. Stone (2013, p. 243) records a senior book buyer at Amazon saying that 'typically it was about thirty days before [the publisher would] come back and say, Ouch, how do we make this work?' This kind of manipulation is perhaps the most compelling evidence that algorithms serve particular ends, ones that are never made transparent to users, who may be misapprehending the recommendations as mirrors of themselves or unmediated expressions of the preferences of a community of readers.

And this is where the biggest difference between human and algorithmic bookselling lies: in the ability to tell us *why*. Algorithmic if-then logic is not the same as the logic of cause-and-effect. If a reader buys Book A and then Book B, this doesn't mean that buying Book A caused the user to buy Book B. Algorithms cannot know why the reader bought Book B, just that there now exists a correlation between buying Book B and Book A (Fletcher, 2021, p. 16). If, based on this correlation, it now recommends Book C, it can't tell us why we should read Book C. This is because, as Smith (2019, p. 208) writes, '*for algorithms, meaning doesn't exist only information does*'. Even when algorithmic prediction beats human editors in choosing which books will be more popular, it can't, unlike the humans, tell us *why* they think this (Bhaskar, 2016). This often doesn't matter: who cares if algorithms don't understand *why* we buy toothpaste and toothbrushes together. But when it comes to books, in which it is often the meaning we are primarily interested in (see the imperfect librarians at the start of this Element), meaning matters. There are many times when it matters much more than in bookselling, such as when algorithms are used to recommend jail sentences, police beats, insurance risks, and medical treatment plans. But if we agree that the books we read help to shape our understanding of the world we live in, then maybe why we read some books over others matters too.

The Slow Browse; or, Keeping Time with Algorithms

This section has been concerned with the process of discovery when buying books with algorithms. In the brick-and-mortar bookstore, we call this process *browsing*. The English word 'to browse' comes from an Old French word meaning to crop and eat, or to graze on vegetation. It was not until the nineteenth century that the word came to mean 'to examine or look through various books in a library, bookshop, etc., esp. in a casual or leisurely manner'. Ultimately the word's meaning expanded to include the perusal of all sorts of items in a store ('browse, v.', 2016). 'Browse' is akin to words like 'ruminate' which metaphorize the actions of animals (to chew food multiple times to digest it) to describe a slow human action (to turn over repeatedly in the mind).

That the perusal of books was the conduit for the transformation of 'browsing' into a human action, means it was something people must have habitually done slowly and over some time. Jeff Deutsch (2022, p. 136) argues, in fact, that the experience of browsing is the primary product of the good bookstore and that booksellers 'cultivate readers as farmers tend their fields'. This pastoral and spatial metaphor that imagines farmers as nurturing and growing but also disciplining and ordering their reader-seeds is repeated in a slightly different form by Thompson (2021, p. 214) who illustrates the rise of Amazon and online bookselling from the perspective of publishers, who were 'slow to wake up to the fact that readers were migrating to new pastures where others were busily tending the flocks. They struggled to understand the lay of the land'. Here, readers are sheep rather than plants (picking up on the browsing metaphor directly), and those trying to sell books are shepherds rather than farmers, but the bucolic tending of fields or pastures as a metaphor for growing a readership is repeated.

Programmers of algorithms have also plumbed the pastoral for metaphor. Seaver (2022, p. 144) records an image he found repeated in his conversations with programmers: 'learning algorithms are the seeds, data is the soil, and the learned programs are the grown plants. The machine learning expert is like a farmer, sowing the seeds, irrigating and fertilizing the soil, and keeping an eye on the health of the crop, but otherwise staying out of the way'. Elsewhere Seaver mentions the metaphor of the park ranger, guiding visitors through an environment based on their interests, as well as the shepherd, tending his flock. Wendy Chun (2018, p. 61) similarly mentions that the rhizomatic growth of networked clusters in statistical data modelling seems to invite techniques of management like pruning. These shared metaphors point up the similarities in brick-and-mortar and algorithmic bookselling: both envision themselves as enacting what Rosalind Cooper calls pastoral power (cited in Seaver, 2022, p. 153): a power defined by a duty of care and minimal intervention, responsive to the needs of all charges, both as a collective and on the level of the individual. Algorithmic bookselling is not doing something fundamentally new when it manipulates our reading choices (although as I've been arguing, the fact that it does so in ways that resist critique seems important). The similarity is reflected in the fact that we access Amazon through our *browser*, which allows us to peruse online sites at our leisure.

The difference, then, is the privileging of rapidity, a logic seemingly inimical to the ruminating browse. In a bookstore the bookseller, through choices made in the display, is certainly responsible for crafting the browsing environment. In the words of Jean-Luc Nancy (2009, p. 37) 'the election and presentation, the whole argumentative, rhetorical, and encyclopedic apparatus of which the bookstore is the material machine in action, and of which booksellers are the inventive soul, all of that leads to the gesture made by a future reader'. The browser, then, must carve a path through this existing material machine of shelves, like the universal librarians, enacting what Michel de Certeau (1988, p. xviii) would call a *poïēsis* – a making and doing through trajectory. The bookstore itself has no ending and no beginning; it is filled with choices that we make during our browsing.

But browsing with algorithms is designed for targeted efficiency. Algorithms show a limited number of options and respond to human inputs with another set of options designed to get us to a felicitous destination. Although the paths seem infinite, they are quite constrained. If you see four recommendations on each page, it will take you twenty-five clicks to see one hundred books (some of which may repeat due to algorithms' attempts to personalize their results). It will take you far fewer than twenty-five paces to peruse one hundred books in a bookstore. The reader as imagined by Amazon is not an ambling flaneur but a 'rational consumer, out to obtain desired goods at the lowest possible cost' (Miller, 2006, p. 17) in terms of both price and time spent. In this model, readers become, like algorithms, rational machines— weighing factors and optimizing results. Although book buyers frequent online bookstores at a higher rate than traditional bookstores (likely due to convenience and cost of travel) they generally spend a shorter time on each visit (Laing and Royle, 2013), leading to a notable decrease in serendipitous impulse buying (Milliot, 2011; Thompson, 2021, p. 258). When used by programmers, pastoral metaphors elide the slow time of seasonal or meteorological cycles that are out of the control of the metaphorical farmers. The seeds planted by programmers are subject only to the cycles of data collection, not to the time it takes their charges to read a book or carve a path through a bookstore.

It would, perhaps, be too much to point to the 'slow, or immersive, time' (Deutsch, 2022, p. 141) of traditional book browsing as the antithesis of or a utopic relief from the ravages of neoliberal speed; however, we should be alert to the fact that selling books with algorithms represents a colonization of a space previously somewhat guarded from this logic (at least in the cultural imaginary). Pressman (2020, p. 24) claims that 'in our neoliberal times, in which digital corporations invade our private space and reading time, claiming a bookish identity can constitute an act of rebellion, self-construction, and hope within this sphere'. When that bookish identity is shaped by the recommendations of bookselling algorithms, autonomous self-construction is less ensured.

4 Making the Invisible Visible

Amazon's algorithms are about making the invisible visible, and, in 2015, Amazon literalized this mission by doing something that all its now shuttered competitors had done before it: opened brick-and-mortar stores. These bookstores were surprisingly small, contradicting Amazon's tagline, 'Earth's Biggest Bookstore'. The Columbus Circle store in New York featured only 3,000 titles (Tolentino, 2017). However, it maintained much of its online identity by orienting books face out, displaying the cover (rather than the spine), like a thumbnail as an advertisement for the book. Beneath each book was a card, not unlike the handwritten ones often accompanying books in independent stores, but these were printed and featured the book's Amazon ranking and a review by an Amazon customer. The organization of the store made material the collaborative filtering algorithms of the site, with local sections featuring top selling books from the city the store was located in, and displays telling you that if you liked one face out book you'd also enjoy the face out book next to it. Titles were swapped out weekly based on updated data. Customers could only purchase books in the store by downloading the Amazon app, which allowed for up-to-the-minute pricing changes (digital price tags in the store updated pricing as often as five times a day (Romano, 2019)) as well as the opportunity to harvest the customer's data, even when they were making purchases in the 'real world' (Thompson, 2021, pp. 191–193). Amazon bookstores were an experiment in combining the experience of browsing in a physical space with the semi-personal curation made possible by Amazon's data.

The experiment ended in early 2022 when Amazon announced the closure of all 68 of its brick-and-mortar locations. Their lack of success was perhaps because the small stores featured none of the "wild cards, deep cuts, and oddballs" customers could find in an independent bookstore (Tolentino, 2017), while also failing to offer the type of felicitous self-recognition afforded by the hyper-personalized algorithmic selections on Amazon's site.

Amazon's brick-and-mortar stores briefly made visible the invisible collecting and processing of data that occurs on its servers. This process – usually hidden by the interface of Amazon's site – is invisible, but it is not immaterial. The contrast between the products Amazon makes visible and its seemingly invisible material effects constitutes a leitmotif of Amazon's operations. For example, Amazon attempts to colonize e-retail across all sectors and products, as well as countless sources of user data, while retaining a very small visible footprint in consumers' lives. Although users may have Ring cameras, Alexa speakers, and standing subscriptions for Amazon products, ideally these are so integrated into the user's everyday experience that they have become invisible. There is (usually) no store to enter and no salesperson to interact with; there is only an occasional and fleeting encounter with an Amazon branded delivery truck, or a view of a warehouse from the highway. This contradiction is made manifest in the friction between the company's tagline, 'the everything store', and Bezos's naming of it as 'the unstore'. At once everywhere and nowhere, the company's many material effects, and not only on the bookselling industry, seem to dissipate into air when traced back to their source. This is often because these real-world effects have been engineered by the socio-technological assemblages that are algorithms, which launder human agency, cleansing it of its potential ethical concerns and providing it with the alibi of quantification.

This is true of Amazon's environmental effects, which are all but invisible to consumers on Amazon's website, hidden by a vocabulary (e.g. 'cloud', 'network', 'platform') that seems ethereal and unrooted from earthly concerns. Their real impacts, however, are simply geographically removed. For example, although the concept of data mining is somewhat misleading as it makes data appear as though it is a natural resource, computation does require the mining of natural resources, primarily lithium, from the earth's crust. Lithium-ion batteries are essential not only for powering our devices, but they also 'undergird the internet and every commerce platform that runs on it'. Lithium, which is in increasingly short supply, is mined in Nevada, central Congo, Mongolia, Indonesia, Western Australia, and southwest Bolivia (the richest site of lithium in the world), and is subject to political tensions over mining rights (Crawford, 2021, pp. 30–32).

Data centres are one of the world's biggest consumers of electricity, and computation on infrastructures like Amazon Web Services produces an enormous carbon footprint, a term which usefully connotes a visible impression left by an invisible actor. Rather than working on more elegant, less environmentally taxing solutions, machine learning algorithms are often trained using a brute force approach, using as much data, and entering as many computational cycles as possible. Corporations are primarily concerned with economic cost and speed, rather than taking into account the marginal environmental costs of high-computational solutions to problems (Crawford, 2021, pp. 43–44).

The feedback loops that power machine learning algorithms also exist in our ecosystem. Currently, the world's data centres use about 3 per cent of the world's electricity and account for 2 per cent of global emissions (about the same as the airline industry). As global temperatures rise due to increased greenhouse gases, data centres will need to expend more and more energy to keep from overheating (Bridle, 2018, p. 63). Estimates suggest that the technology sector will be responsible for 14 per cent of global greenhouse emissions by 2040, and that data centres alone will increase their electricity demands fifteen-fold by 2030 (Crawford, 2021, p. 42). In 2019, 1,000 Amazon workers cited its massive carbon footprint in the company's first ever white-collar walkout (Crawford, 2021, p. 85).

One benefit of Amazon's seeming immateriality is its ability to bypass national censorship regimes. Censorship often relies on physical points of entry, and embargoes are efficient at keeping out large shipments of books. Censored books are easy to see and remove in brick-and-mortar bookstores. But censorship is much harder to enforce when readers buy individual books online. A study (Tella, Uwaifo, and Akande, 2021, p. 13) of postgraduate students in Nigeria who use online bookstores like Amazon found that students appreciated being able to buy books that were not available in bookstores. 'Ordering books online', one student says, 'has cancelled and rendered the embargo useless and unworkable'. Customs officers stop large shipments ordered by bookstores or wholesalers, but they can't inspect every individual book ordered online, and it remains legal, at least in Nigeria, for individuals to buy embargoed books as long as they are not sold.

Even when censorship is not in effect, the appearance of books where there previously were none is undoubtedly a material effect of selling books online. Readers in remote areas, where there are neither enough buyers nor employees to support a brick-and mortar bookstore benefit from being able to order books remotely. Erik Brynjolfsson and Michael D. Smith (2003) calculated that at the turn of the millennium, the average consumer in the US lived 5.4 miles from the nearest bookstore while 14 per cent lived further than 10 miles away and 8 per cent lived more than 20 miles away. Beyond just giving these consumers access to the long tail, the automation of algorithmic bookselling makes *all* books more accessible to these readers. While Amazon, at least in part, helped in creating these book deserts by competing with small bookstores on price, selection, and convenience, the fact remains that online bookselling makes books easily accessible in places where they were not before.

This new access to books is facilitated by a shift in different types and locations of labour, much of it now made invisible to the buyers of books. This is in large part because the labour is taking place not in a local bookstore, but in a warehouse – usually near enough to a city to take advantage of a large employee pool, but far enough away to avoid high rents. Much discussion surrounding AI and machine learning is concerned with whether algorithms might replace human workers, what types of jobs they might do, and how long it will be until the costs of producing these algorithms will be cheaper than paying human workers. Algorithms have already redistributed the labour of bookselling. In the sections that follow, I'll trace some of the ways this is happening from the perspective of the online Amazon user, the bookseller, and the 'warehouse associate' – the Amazon employees, often working through subcontracted employment agencies, who stock and ship the books that arrive at customers' doors. This section aims, like Amazon's experimental storefronts, to make the invisible visible by considering some of the material effects on labour of selling books with algorithms.

The User as Labourer

Amazon's algorithms work by processing large amounts of data, data that is produced primarily through the clicks, scrolls, purchases, ratings, and reviews of its users (and users on Goodreads and its other affiliate sites).

In effect, the profit Amazon reaps by supplanting the labour of booksellers who find and recommend books is made possible through a combination of the work of paid programmers and the 'unpaid contributions of its users' (Srinivasan, 2017, p. 22) who devote some of their time to freely fuelling algorithms and therefore the profitability of Amazon.

We could argue that users do this because it benefits them as well. Users enter, as Astrid Mager (2012, p. 10) writes, an 'alliance' to reach their own goal of conveniently finding a book, while incidentally providing data to algorithms and making a profit for Amazon. This type of user behaviour – of collectively producing (or 'crowdsourcing') information that remains freely accessible, such as on rating and review sites or Wikipedia – has a long history on the internet. Amazon then monetizes this behaviour, and it does so without paying users. When Goodreads users 'shelve' books, they provide Amazon with data about that book and also about themselves as customers (Walsh and Antoniak, 2021). Although some argue that value isn't created by the users producing data, but by the manipulation and computation of that data, Valerie Jarrett (2022, p. 23) insists that it is the fact that value is extracted 'from user contributions that transforms such activity from work – activity creating objects with embedded, meaningful value to the user (use-value) – into labour – activity producing goods defined primarily by their value in a marketplace (exchange-value)'. This is the trade-off of shopping on Amazon: buying often heavily discounted products with convenient shipping times in exchange for the free use of unpaid labour.

This is where the 'data mining' metaphor begins to fall apart somewhat. The metaphor is meaningful because it compares companies like Amazon with the industrialists of the manufacturing economies of past centuries, who extracted value from the land through mining, logging, industrial agriculture, and digging and fracking for oil or gas. In these industries, profits came from exploiting naturally occurring resources (as well as, usually, underpaid labour). Data, although often traded as a commodity, is not naturally occurring. 'To talk about data like water, gold, or oil is to hide data's connections to all the people whose activities produce it', as Seaver (2022, p. 146) writes, 'figuring it instead as the untainted, objective stuff of the outside world, innocent of human politics and concerns'. Data is created through what we might call our informational, creative, or social labour, and then recorded by our devices (Lamdan, 2022). That this can be done at all times – while wearing digital watches or phones, or through recording devices in our homes – signifies a complete collapse between the labouring and private worlds of the individual: we are nearly always producing value for online platforms like Amazon, which are always prepared to capture that value (Jarrett, 2022). The term data mining occludes the fact that it is not the contemporary tech companies like Amazon who are labouring (or paying labourers) to extract data, but that it is the customers of those companies who are doing the work. Data isn't so much mined as it is captured before it melts into air.

End User License Agreements and Terms of Service define the relationship between users and the companies that extract value from their data. Although user labour is certainly exploited by Amazon, users do have relative autonomy. They are not required to work set hours or produce a certain number of clicks. In fact, they are not required to work at all. And there are very few rules about how users should work while they are working (although there are incitements to work in certain ways; algorithms, as I've already discussed, subtly work to discipline user behaviours in ways that produce the most value).

However, there remains little transparency about how user data is used and how users' actions implicate them in a larger system of value production. An example of the difficulty of imagining users as labourers is made somewhat more visible in the rise of fast food ordering kiosk and grocery self check out lanes. It appears as though these machines have replaced the worker with automation, when what they have really done is relocate the site of labour from the paid employee to the unpaid customer (Crawford, 2021).

As we've seen before, selling books with algorithms comes down to time and speed. Bezos's 2020 shareholder letter claims that 28 per cent of purchases on Amazon are made in three minutes or less, pointing to the extreme convenience this shopping environment provides. 50 per cent of purchases are made in less than a quarter of an hour. 'Compare that', Bezos urges, 'to the typical shopping trip to a physical store – driving, parking, searching store aisles, waiting in the checkout line, finding your car, and driving home'. Bezos tells us that research suggests 'the typical physical store trip takes about an hour'. He calculates that Amazon saves the average consumer about seventy-five hours a year (Bezos, 2021). But the calculation that is missing here is that this average consumer will have provided Amazon with thirteen hours of unpaid data production in this year, and that's just time spent shopping on the site. Bezos, whose company made over $380 billion in 2020, ends this part of his letter by acknowledging that, yes, 'we're all busy in the early 21st century'. Some people just get paid more for their time than others.

The Work of Selling Books: Selection, Pricing, and Marketing

The work that is being replaced by the algorithmic collaboration of users and programmers is the work of bookselling. Recent changes wrought by the superstores and Amazon, which have forced even small bookstores to rationalize – decreasing salaries and retaining the minimum possible staff – have changed labour dynamics in the bookstore. Bookstore employees don't command high salaries, and, as Steiner (2017) writes, while bookselling used to be an attractive profession, it now often acts as temporary employment for people like college students. Although bookstore staff are often more educated than other retail employees, and often have a personal interest in the products they are selling, they seldom see their jobs as long-term careers. While much of this likely has to do with the low material compensation of bookstore positions, it may also be due to the increased automation even in brick-and-mortar stores. The human skill and discretion once required for keeping a store up to date and attractively stocked are now often wholly or partially automated. Even the act of providing an in-store recommendation has been facilitated by the data generated by point of sale systems and customer cards or phone numbers used to track past purchases. Although that data isn't algorithmically processed like the data captured on Amazon's sites, it still displaces some of the creative labour once required by human booksellers.

Much of this Element has been focused on algorithmic recommendations and search functions. This is because this is the sometimes magical work of bookselling (and the part of bookselling most difficult to automate). A 1960s guide to bookselling proclaims that 'it is not the bookseller's job to tell the prospective reader what he must read. To do that is to reinforce the trend toward standardization and conformity, which we already have too much of in our daily routine, but it is the bookseller's task to see that the right book is sold to the right person. It is his primary goal to see that the readers he encounters find the book they are seeking and need' (quoted in Miller, 2006, p. 59 note 7). Figuring out what a reader wants (or perhaps what they don't yet know that they want) is work that requires time, ability, effort, empathy, and, most importantly, knowledge.

In this way we might think of human book recommendation as a sort of craft. A recent study (Stauff, van Romondt Vis, & van Es, 2023, p. 37) uses an ethnographic approach to describe the relationship between human craftspeople and their workplace interactions with algorithms in the context of coffee roasting. 'A craft', the authors write, 'implies careful attention to and knowledge about the raw materials one works with'. In coffee roasting, this means understanding different types of beans, what temperatures to roast them at and for how long, adjusting for changes in air temperature or the water content of the beans. Although modern algorithmic coffee roasters can be programmed to do the task autonomously, ultimately it is the craftsperson who knows how a particular bean and roast are supposed to taste (and even sound the beans should make as they are roasting), and who takes pleasure in manipulating the machine to produce a more felicitous output.

The raw material for the bookseller is the book – its content, not its metadata. The recommendation the bookseller makes is a reflection of his personal taste, but also a projection of what others might enjoy made from a position of 'local, embodied, and qualitatively rich human subjectivity' as opposed to a 'distant and aggregating objectivity' (Stauff, van Romondt Vis, and van Es, 2023, p. 36). The knowledge deployed by booksellers is both object directed and intersubjective. In this sense human book recommendation is a social act, one that, in Danielle Fuller and DeNel Rehberg Sedo's (2023, p. 62) account, generates 'social pleasure derived from moments of interpersonal communication that are sometimes about identification and that, at other times, register as curiosity and interest: a pleasure of responding in relation to others'. This is not to say that book recommendation is somehow a utopic act, but rather that it can produce something of value outside of a purely economic logic.

In addition to making recommendations, a task of the bookseller is figuring out what to stock and returning unsold stock to publishers for a refund. When deciding what to stock, booksellers evaluate factors including sales of authors' previous works, the popularity of various genres, the publishers' marketing reach, the ease of ordering, and the relevant costs of books (Miller, 2006, p. 69). As has been the topic of much of this book, the weighting of these factors, which once required a great amount of knowledge and discernment as well as presenting an opportunity for bias and discrimination, is now done instantaneously by algorithms. Amazon's just-in-time distribution system means that algorithms calculate which books to stock in which of its global warehouses, predicting ordering patterns and decreasing occupied shelf space. This is doubtlessly more efficient; Amazon returns less than 5 per cent of unsold stock to publishers, whereas big book chains regularly return up to 40 per cent of unsold stock (Stone, 2013).

In traditional bookselling, pricing was not a central concern. Books came with a list price from the publisher and were sold to merchants at a standard discount based on the type of book. This discount became the bookseller's margin upon the sale of the book, with which they would pay for their rent, overhead, and salary costs. Booksellers would only have to worry about pricing when organizing special sales. In the US rarely are books sold at the list price on Amazon. (In some countries fixed book price laws make it illegal to change the retail price of books, even on Amazon, in order to avoid downward pressure on books with the aim of protecting small, independent bookstores (Thomas, 2019, p. 404)). Although every book has a single page on Amazon's US site, several sellers can list their copies for sale, all at different prices. This introduces an aspect of labour new to algorithmic bookselling: determining, sometimes for each individual copy, at what price buyers will want to buy the book while providing the seller with the largest possible profit.

Other than for the smaller sellers, humans are not the ones undertaking this labour. Sellers on Amazon who trade in large quantities of books (including Amazon itself) use price setting algorithms that run several times a day to adjust the prices of their books. Other algorithms, created by Amazon, determine which seller's copy and price to display in the 'Buy

Box', a prominent section of the book page which lists the best (i.e. cheapest and fastest) combination of price and delivery speed (see Figure 5). Sellers' price setting algorithms, then, are trained to try to achieve selection for the 'Buy Box'. A recent study found that sellers who use algorithms to price their books have higher sales volume than sellers who don't (Chen, Mislove, and Wilson, 1340). Contrary, perhaps, to expectation, Amazon itself does not always win the Buy Box, but it ranks in the top five sellers

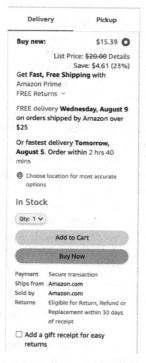

Figure 5 The buy box for the paperback Penguin edition of Volume 1 of Karl Marx's *Capital* (list price $20.00) on 4 August 2023. Although there are ninety other copies for sale, Amazon has won the buy box for the moment.

88 per cent of the time. And it is well known that Amazon is happy to treat books as 'loss leaders', which means that they make low or no profits on books to entice users to buy other, more profitable items on its site (Deutsch 7). Although algorithmic pricing often leads to lower prices than the recommended list price, which is a boon for consumers, it also increases uncertainty for buyers, who may find that the price of a book varies widely from day to day. Barring Amazon bookstores' digital price read-outs, it would be nearly impossible to translate this kind of algorithmic pricing into brick-and-mortar stores, as it would exponentially increase the labour of the bookseller, who would need to be constantly updating the current price of each book.

We might consider the competing pricing algorithms that aim to help sellers gain visibility in the marketplace a type of systems gaming. Systems gaming is a term that describes the actions users and programmers take to 'game' algorithms – to take advantage of their operation for personal gain. Systems gaming means to optimize one's behaviour to better suit the desires of algorithms. Some consider those who game the system to be operating in bad faith (since algorithms are supposed to reflect, not determine our actions), while others see acts of systems gaming as a natural response to the existence of algorithmic mediators (Petre, Duffy, and Hund, 2019). For example, publishers might enter metadata using terms that they know will provide more hits, even if those terms aren't ones that best describe the book in question. Platforms like Amazon usually frown upon acts of systems gaming because they belie the fact that algorithmic outputs are manipulable and can be changed to advantage specific players. Amazon does not pay the publishers for entering book metadata (a source of data that again seems to be simply mined, but is really produced, at a cost, by the publishing industry).

Systems gaming also occurs when favourable reviews are written by the author or publisher of a book or when negative reviews are written by a competitor. The threat of inaccurate or bad faith reviews is so great for Amazon that it has invested in several technical checks to discourage them, including creating 'verified purchase' tags, elevating reviews with that tag in the list of visible reviews (Murray, 2018, p. 135), and creating an additional layer of metrics by allowing users to rate whether they find reviews 'helpful' or not. These actions are a way of disciplining the new types of labour that selling books with algorithms creates. As self-published authors often discover, the seeming democracy of algorithms is undermined by the fact that it costs a lot of money to figure out how to use algorithms to one's advantage in marketing a new book. Publishers and marketing companies invest time and money in order to position books in a way that will make them visible to search and recommendation algorithms, and individuals or smaller companies often can't compete.

When systems gaming doesn't work, hacking does. In 2017 the self-published novel *Dragonsoul* moved from its ranking at 385,841 to number one on Amazon's top seller chart. The author used click farms, which work almost like automated sweatshops, creating clicks in the absence of any actual readers, to make it appear as though the book was being downloaded and paged through repeatedly. In this instance, even the reader's work of reading is replaced, at least in the view of algorithms, who'll inform you that 'users like you' bought *Dragonsoul* even when those 'users' are a line of code programmed to iterate endlessly (King, 2019, p. 426).

This narrative about automation in bookselling makes it seem that while the demand for bookselling labour is decreasing, it is being steadily replaced by a need for programmers. But this is not the case. As Stone reports, an Amazon project called 'Hands Off the Wheel' has as its aim the progressive automation of the entire site. At first, software was made responsible for placing purchase orders, then it took over the distribution of products across its warehouses. Now, algorithms negotiate terms with vendors, and marketing employees are no longer necessary to facilitate other companies' brand campaigns on the site. The aim, Stone writes, is to turn 'Amazon's retail business into a largely self-service technology platform that could generate cash with minimum human intervention' (2021, p. 165). Eventually, Amazon's aim is to decrease the number of workers, including programmers, whose labour it relies on, depending instead on the data it is freely 'mining', and its low-pay manual labourers, whose work is hidden in its distribution centres around the world.

Making Rate

While algorithms on Amazon discipline the labour of users as they navigate the site, they do so at the will of the user, who can log off at any time without penalty. This is not the case with the workers at Amazon distribution centres, whose work is regimented by algorithms that dictate their paths through the shelves, tally minutes not working, and optimize their movements (Smith, 2019, p. 141). Emily Guendelsberger, a journalist who worked as a seasonal associate during 'peak' (a word describing the high sales season from November through January), writes that the first thing 'pickers' do when they enter the warehouse is pick up a scan gun, which communicates the location of products to workers while collecting data and tracking workers' locations (even as workers take trips to the bathroom, which are labelled 'time off task' (Evans, 2019)). Guendelsberger (2019, pp. 11, 48) records that she walked up to sixteen miles per day, tracking down objects in the shelves as the LCD screen on the scan gun showed 'a blue bar … that gets shorter and shorter as your remaining seconds tick by'. Speed is the name of the game.

Products, including books, are distributed across the warehouse, each with a scannable bar code. Their arrangement on the shelves, unlike that of a bookstore, is not designed to be navigable by people. This is called random distribution and is determined by algorithms that weight factors like frequency of orders and the size and shape of items along with what items are often purchased together. Although the result of a computed 'best' output, item locations seem random to human understanding and may change without notice. This makes the warehouse 'computationally efficient, but makes it completely incomprehensible to humans' (Bridle, 2018, p. 116), who – in stark contrast to the *poēisis* of the browser in the bookstore – need to rely on the scan gun to direct all of their movements. Heike Geissler (2018, p. 70), a writer who, like Guendelsberger, worked as a seasonal associate, records a manager telling her 'you don't have to understand it, by the way, you just have to know it'. Although this statement reflects the dehumanization of the worker in the warehouse, who is told to simply rely on algorithmic outputs rather than her own comprehension, it is just as applicable to the site's user, who is asked not to think so much about why books are being recommended, but to simply accept that these books are suitable.

Algorithms seemingly know and control everything in the distribution centre. A group of machine learning algorithms called 'the matrix', tells workers which boxes or mailers are optimum for the size, shape, and weight of the objects they are packing. If a customer marks an object as 'damaged in transit', the matrix recalculates its recommendation for that object, which is then relayed to the workers in the distribution centre, meaning that they are 'forced to continually adapt, which makes it harder to put their knowledge into action or habituate to the job' (Crawford, 2021, p. 56). Algorithms also draw up workers' schedules: predicting how many employees will be needed for how long. Unsurprisingly, they don't seem to weight the convenience of the worker, contiguous sleep hours, or childcare needs highly in their list of relevant factors (Guendelsberger, 2019, p. 9).

The most important data points gathered in the warehouses are the number of products successfully unpacked from incoming deliveries, 'picked' from the warehouse shelves, or packaged for outgoing delivery to customers. When added up and divided by a unit of time, this is called 'the rate', and is a productivity measure calculated by a proprietary software system called ADAPT (Evans, 2019). The rate is an ever-changing target computed both for individuals and entire shifts, which means that workers are encouraged to pressure each other to perform faster. If a worker's rate is repeatedly low, they are reprimanded and eventually risk being fired. Workers report skipping bathroom breaks to make rate (unlike Borges's universal library, commodes are not conveniently placed in the corridors for easy access). Managers some-times 'revoke talking privileges' until workers start making rate, which can be tracked in real time using the data produced by the scan guns (Guendelsberger, 2019, p. 48). By disciplining or firing workers who don't make rate, some factories are able to hit coveted targets, which are celebrated with commem-orative t-shirts, like at the Eastvale factory in California which recently hit a million packages processed in twenty-four hours (Evans, 2019).

The algorithmically processed and produced 'rate', which adjusts according to various inputs, is the flip side of the recommendation algo-rithms on Amazon's site. Although they are weighting different inputs, both optimize human behaviour according to logics of speed: how fast can you show a user the book they will buy, or how fast can you get a human to find and package a book. Geissler's description of her trainer at the warehouse in Leipzig shows this optimization in action: 'Norman's movements follow a strict sense of timing; he seems to use the exact amount of time for each activity, everything is subordinated to his sense of time, and each product to be processed is merely something that impairs the adherence to time requirements more or less than others' (2018, p. 69). Here objects like books become not even commodities representing exchange value, but simply, through their material existence, physical barriers to speed.

Even though Amazon started out primarily as a bookseller, the time of the Amazon distribution centre is the antithesis of reading time. Geissler treats the job as market research, becoming familiar with the reading tendencies of German customers, noting the popularity of the humorous health writer Eckart von Hirschhausen and the 'incredible number of vampire novels' (2018, p. 61). But after Geissler is chastised for reading when she should be scanning (i.e. letting the computer read the barcode) she writes:

> You're not inherently against optimization, either; you just don't usually think of optimizing actions. I've never taken a course in speed-reading or speed-typing. Still, you attempt to make more effort, you stop examining books, you're only interested in speed; it's a kind of downhill race. You make yourself thin, reject all temptation to open up one of the books. But after half an hour you lose focus and then you do open up another books, reading a few lines and relaxing.

Unlike Sumpter, who collapses the distinction between the subject 'known' by algorithms and the one who connects to a novel, Geissler's use of both the first- and second-person reveals that the 'rate' and the books themselves are hailing two different subjects: one is the alienated subject of algorithmic work-time, and the other is the subject engaged in the slow-time of reading.

The logic of speed in selling books with algorithms makes its most brutal mark on the bodies of Amazon employees. As we've seen, 'the control over time is a consistent theme in the Amazon logistical empire' and, as Crawford (2021, p. 56) adds, 'the bodies of workers are run according to the cadences of computational logics'. It is in the distribution centres where the time it takes to move objects through space and across distance (in the visible world) meets the algorithmic time of nearly instantaneous decisions made by clicks and computations (in the invisible world). Where these worlds meet they produce friction, usually at the cost of the worker. Repetitive motion and strain injuries are so common in the warehouses that Amazon provides free vending machines stocked with over-the-counter painkillers. These were introduced after lines at the medical office made it difficult to navigate through key corridors in the warehouse.

After workers in a Minnesota warehouse walked out, Amazon came to the negotiating table to discuss workplace conditions but said that it would not be able to discuss changing the rate, which was determined algorithmically and therefore not subject to human intervention (a common appeal to the objectivity of algorithms). If a single warehouse negotiated a different rate it would threaten Amazon's entire ordering of time, throwing the warehouses out of sync (Crawford, 2021, p. 84). The rate, in this sense, like Greenwich Mean Time before it, consolidates the power of Amazon into a global daily rhythm. Amazon is, according to Bezos (2021) himself, 'developing new automated staffing schedules that use sophisticated algorithms to rotate employees among jobs that use different muscle-tendon groups to decrease repetitive motion'. In addition, Amazon has bought Kiva, a robotics company, in order to develop automated robots that will move between pickers and packers, limiting the number of miles walked by humans each day (Stone, 2021, p. 222).

Despite the transparency in Amazon's warehouses – the availability of the location of all items and employees, the immediate calculation of 'the rate' which can be used to change disciplinary tactics in real time – algorithms in Amazon's warehouses continue to trade in strategic practices of invisibility. Despite the number of pickers and the miles they each walk, Guendelsberger (2019, p. 52) rarely encountered other employees during her shifts: 'whatever algorithm plots our pick paths around the warehouse is brilliantly engineered, immensely complicated and set to keep people from getting within speaking distance of one another'. This strategic invisibility (despite the place being 'swarming with pickers during pick', Guendelsberger is rarely 'close enough to another human long enough to say hello'), makes it difficult for workers to communicate or share information. Despite generating the information that makes the warehouse algorithms work, workers are unable to share their own information about, for example, safety concerns, their body aches and pains, or their need to use the bathroom or sit down for a moment. This is a well-known affordance of corporate algorithms, found also by workers at Uber: by controlling your movements, 'the technology ... effectively precludes you from working with your colleagues for the advancement of working conditions' (Bridle, 2018, p. 116). Similarly, despite Amazon's obsession with metrics, during the COVID-19 pandemic it declined to release statistics about positive cases. Jana Jumpp, a former employee in Indiana gathered the data she could on confirmed cases on a shared Google spreadsheet, citing a desire for visibility. 'I want them to know', she says, 'that there's somebody counting'. At Amazon algorithms are always already counting: products, seconds, products per second. But the well-being of employees, although measured in serious injuries per 100 (9.6 in 2018, compared to an industry average that year of 4 (Evans, 2019)), does not seem to be weighted heavily by these algorithms.

But algorithms still require human compliance to work. Guendelsberger (2019, p. 90) reports that workers hated being assigned to the fourth floor of the Louisville warehouse she was working in. The fourth floor held oversized items, meaning the distance between picks was longer and workers needed to take more trips to the conveyor belt to drop off their items. 'I almost never make rate on the fourth floor', she writes, which is why she was disappointed to find that she was almost always assigned the fourth floor when she logged into her scan gun. It turns out that the other pickers had been logging out and back in until they drew a non-fourth floor assignment. This practice, which elicited scolding from management, is a type of systems gaming in which humans 'optimize' their behaviour to manipulate algorithms. Similarly, Geissler witnessed the early shift gaming the system at the cost of other shifts: the forklift drivers delivered only the best, non-complicated packages to their colleagues, who processed them quickly, increasing the shift's overall productivity. This meant that the problem products were left for the other shifts, who found it more difficult to make rate (Geissler, 2018, pp. 174–175). In the warehouse, these tactics are shaped in response to algorithms, reversing the direction of the gaze: from algorithms-watching-workers to workers-watching-algorithms.

Although selling books with algorithms appears to buyers as a seamless interaction taking place at roughly the speed and materiality of light, this is because the material effects of bookselling have been displaced. When attempting to circumvent censorship regimes, Amazon's invisibility is a boon, but when it obscures the labour conditions in distribution centres and the environmental impacts of computation, it alienates buyers from the effects of their clicks and purchases. Although brick-and-mortar stores don't avoid all these pitfalls, it is important, I think, to make visible what selling books with algorithms removes from our immediate consciousness in order to consider whose time it is that is being saved, and how this algorithmic revolution has transformed our relationship to the world and to each other.

5 Future Directions

Many of the tensions that arise from selling books with algorithms also exist where algorithms are applied to other realms of human judgment including law, economics, healthcare, and education, with more severe and immediate consequences. While the book industry might seem a frivolous arena in comparison, I would make a modest claim that what we read matters because, like algorithmic outputs, our reading iteratively shapes our understanding of the world we live in. Some of the shortcomings of algorithmic understandings of us that I've been describing here – an inability to account for change, a sense of humans as data profiles that are disciplined into legible categories – are precisely the issues that literature and the arts (broadly folded under the umbrella of the humanities) are particularly suited to grapple with.

Algorithms' sense of uncertainty, from which stems their potential to generate surprise, discovery, uncanniness, and the bizarre, comes from the gap between reality and the world that it has modelled using statistics. Whether or not the next click reaffirms or recomputes that reality is constantly in question. But humans have to account for other types of generative uncertainty including semantic uncertainty (what does this book or this algorithmic recommendation mean) and ontological uncertainty (what sorts of new things might I discover and how can I make them accord with my existing understanding of the world) (Smith, 2019, p. 209). Literature makes these types of uncertainty visible and generates meaning from them, whereas algorithms ignore them: why a data proxy might correlate with an outcome is not important; objects or actions that aren't captured by data don't exist; outliers are statistically insignificant and shouldn't change our understanding of the world. This logic is antithetical to literature, whose aim, so often, is to describe specific, idiosyncratic relationships between the one and the many: how are actions derived from emotions; what methods should we use to understand things that we have never encountered before; if everyone is an outlier, is anyone? Books' uniqueness (no two, as Bezos himself determined, are the same) rhymes with the aims of book history and bibliography, which afford the study of '*the individuality of all things, every instance, every copy'* (Kirschenbaum, 2021, p. 111). This contrasts starkly with the modelling impulse of algorithms in which each data point must be made commensurable.

One thing that books and algorithms share is their opacity and need for interpretation. We could reimagine Borges's universal library not as a library, but as a book, whose readers search endlessly for the kernel of meaning that will free them from their search. Readers of books often see this quest for meaning as part of reading's pleasure; for some, the more ambiguous the text the better. Yet, at least in this stage of our social uptake of algorithms, users seem to resist applying those same critical faculties to algorithmic results. Perhaps this is because of the 'automation bias' that I've discussed, which 'ensures that we value automated information more highly than our own experiences, even when it conflicts with other observations – particularly when those observations are ambiguous' (Bridle, 2018, p. 40). When we unquestioningly accept, for example, a book recommendation from an algorithm that we would not accept from a human, we privilege a (datafied, computational) view of ourselves, operating within a particular logic (of speed and optimization). Bridle suggests that this is because of time pressure: algorithms offer a 'computational hack' for cognitive effort that tasks like reading, or selecting books require. His solution is to insist on a type of algorithmic literacy that recognizes that the world is not computable, yet often shaped in irrevocable ways by computation.

What might it mean for users to become better readers of algorithms? To read them in the way that we read literature, which, as Sumpter says, feels like a personal conversation, rather than to just accept their dictates? Perhaps becoming better readers of algorithms would mean, to return to the epigraphs of this Element, coming to understand that algorithms are not mirrors of the world, but of ourselves and our understanding of it, and that in using them to access that world, we remain responsible for shaping it.

This would require a demystification of algorithms as a technology. As Ramesh Srinivasan (2017, p. 45) writes, technologies like algorithms are not 'universal or mystical'. They are material: 'created by people and therefore potentially open to human modification, creativity, and appropriation'. This might mean putting social pressure on corporations to reveal how their algorithms use data and statistical modelling to produce outputs or developing new ways of assessing and acting with or against algorithmic recommendations. As Chun bracingly writes:

> It is critical that we realize that the gap between prediction and reality is the space for political action and agency . . . . Like global climate change and human population models, [predictions] can point to realities and futures to be rejected. They can, through their diagnosis, render impotent the predictive power of a symptom or enable new, unforeseen, grammars. To create new expressions, however, we need to read the scripts and analyze the set we find ourselves in the midst of. (2008, p. 68)

In the language of this Element, this means acknowledging that algorithmic recommendations, like literature, do not come to us as true or untrue, but that we have the power to assign a recommendation's felicitousness through our interpretation.

Although algorithms do wield considerable ideological force, it remains the case that users do not need to and often don't just 'sheepishly take whatever is recommended to them or trust in an algorithm's authority no matter what its output' (Cohn, 2019, p. 124). Although, and because we are so deeply implicated in and intertwined with the functioning of algorithms (Bucher, 2018, p. 154), we have the ability and maybe even the responsibility to be aware of how and why we are interacting with algorithms (interactions that produce new data that will then recursively shape the future outputs presented to others). But the consciousness of this responsibility is not yet widespread. As Cheney-Lippold (2017, p. 30) writes, 'we lack the vocabulary to enact a politics around our algorithmic identities'. While some actions, such as increasing privacy settings and intentionally clicking outside of top-rated results have been suggested (Amrollahi and McBride, 2019), a large-scale consideration of how we might popularly mobilize our labour while producing data in a politically conscious way is something future studies might take into consideration.

But this responsibility should not be ours alone to tackle as individuals. Just like recycling does not solve the systemic problems of the depletion of natural resources or greenhouse emissions, neither do personal privacy settings ameliorate the larger issues of data exploitation (Lamdan, 2022, p. 23). In 2018, the EU began enforcing the 'General Data Protection Regulation' (GDPR), which fines corporations for their misuse of user data. Although it's not yet clear how or whether this will ultimately affect, for example, the selling of books with algorithms, it does take a step in acknowledging that corporations will not regulate their own data use, and that this use has implications for both individuals and societies (Thompson, 2021, p. 444). The US, with its laissez-faire approach to the economy, has done less to regulate user data, although in May 2023 the Biden-Harris administration released a package of efforts to study and manage the growth of AI in key fields like education. These efforts include an AI Bill of Rights that outlines best practices in the categories of 'safe and effective systems', 'algorithmic discrimination protections', 'data privacy', 'notice and explanation', and 'human alternatives, consideration, and fallback'. 'Too often', the document opens, '[technology, data, and automated systems] are used to limit our opportunities and prevent our access to critical resources or services' (*Blueprint for an AI Bill of Rights*, no date). There is no mechanism yet to enforce these rights, and there is no way of knowing if they will be enforced in what is seen as an at-will economic sphere; however, these efforts show awareness of the need for increased algorithmic literacy at the governmental level and an attempt to reign in ownership of the 'means of cognition' (David M. Berry in Raley and Rhee, 2023, p. 194).

This type of regulation that protects users from poor algorithmic outcomes should extend to the environmental and labour implications of tech companies like Amazon. Just as the environment that computation harms is a commons that requires regulation to protect, we can see (and regulate) the data produced by consumers as a sort of 'commons'—a shared resource owned by no one in particular (O'Shea, 2019, p. 258). Although companies like Amazon often fall back on a narrative that privileges their origins as startups that won out in the free market through the wit and acumen of their fearless CEOs, in fact, the development of algorithmic technology from which these companies derive their profits were publicly subsidized by defence funding and federal research agencies. Furthermore, corporations like Amazon rely heavily on public utilities like fibre-optic cables, roads, and the US postal service, even though they often receive tax breaks from local and state officials in return for providing vote-gaining employment opportunities (Crawford, 2021, pp. 216–217). An Amazon 2022 SWOT report lists as the major threats to Amazon's growth: 'any existing and future law related to taxation, data protection, privacy, pricing, content, distribution, copyrights, transportation, electronic device certification, mobile communications, electronic waste, energy consumption, electronic contracts, environmental regulation and other communications, competition, consumer protection, employment trade and protectionist measures, web services, the provision of online payment services, information reporting requirements'. In other words, any regulation whose logic values something other than Amazon's profits represents a threat to it.

The spread of a political vocabulary and will surrounding the regulation of algorithms becomes more urgent as we look to the future of selling books with algorithms. What happens when systems gaming – changing behaviour to appease algorithms – occurs not only on the level of metadata, but on the level of content? The nonfiction publishing company, Callisto Media, is an example of this. Callisto reviews the search terms suggested by Amazon when users start typing into the search box and finds cases in which that search returns no results. It then commissions and publishes books that would be fitting results for that query. The idea is to pinpoint a demand (in this case shaped by an algorithm that completes search terms) and then fill it. According to the CEO, Benjamin Wayne, editors 'pick a winner' 3 per cent of the time (Althoff, 2016). Similarly, on Kindle Direct Publishing, where users can self-publish books and receive 30 per cent royalties based on the number of pages users turn (McGurl, 2016, p. 450), the logic of algorithmic search and recommendation creates an incentive to make book content easily discoverable and quickly consumable.

This means that writing styles, plots, and vocabularies of novels are being optimized to pay off algorithmically. Tracking the effects of this optimization on literary history will be an on-going task for scholars. Algorithms trained on bestselling novels found that 'a strong, young female protagonist whose most-used verbs are "need" and "want"' when combined with a three-act plotline and a thematic focus on modern technology, jobs and the workplace, and human closeness, provides the best shot at achieving bestseller status. Ironically, the novel this algorithm identified as most optimally meeting these requirements was *The Circle*, a satirical dystopic novel by Dave Eggers about the rise of a powerful internet company that trades in big data (Althoff, 2016). When the main character of *The Circle* is the subject of a demonstration in which her preferences (based on algorithmic outcomes) are shared publicly, she thinks: 'So what had so mortified her during [the] presentation? She couldn't put her finger on it . . .. Was it the pinpoint accuracy of the algorithms? Maybe. But then again, it wasn't entirely accurate, so was *that* the problem? Having a matrix of preferences presented as your essence, as the whole you? Maybe that was it. It was some kind of mirror, but it was incomplete, distorted' (2013, p. 126). In a novel chosen by algorithms as an ideal bestseller, Mae's thoughts about algorithms' relationship to herself echo the conflicts presented in this Element.

The possibility of felicitous and infelicitous outputs continues to hold for AI generated writing, which is also subject to the sort of ideological distortions I've discussed in the context of recommendation and search algorithms. Are these AI generated books, like many of the books in Borges's library, simply 'senseless cacophonies, verbal jumbles and incoherences', or should we ascribe them meaning, as it is within our power to do? With the instantaneity afforded by algorithms, it is even possible that ebooks, like Amazon algorithms, could be tailored in real time in response to the data generated by a human's reading. Although more work in this area is welcome, scholars are busy asking 'what is at stake in 'optimizing' would-be cultural artifacts' (Hallinan and Striphas, 2016, p. 131), and how does statistical modelling of audiences effect (either positively or negatively) diverse representation in cultural production (Havens, 2020, p. 159). Publishers have always been interested in filling gaps in the market and providing readers with what they want, but for all the same reasons that selling books with algorithms should be approached critically, so, too, should the potential for publishing and writing books with algorithms.

Amazon is not the only bookseller that sells books with algorithms. To compete with the e-commerce giant, bookshop.org, a non-profit, donates its revenues back to participating independent bookstores. It, too, uses algorithms to sell books, but it does so to support brick-and-mortar stores, which it calls, 'community hubs that foster culture, curiosity, and a love of reading'. Selling books with algorithms, in this case, is a last-ditch effort, not a preferred avenue, to give 'independent bookstores tools to compete online and financial support to help them maintain their presence in local communities' (Bookshop.org, no date). The 'About Us' page even calls out its main competition in a blurb: 'thanks to Bookshop, there's no need to buy on Amazon anymore'. Although this Element has been focused on Amazon's use of algorithms to sell books, future work might centre subversive or tactical uses of algorithms in bookselling and book recommendation. Algorithms remain limited in the ways they describe the world and how they configure user and book data, and algorithmic literacy remains crucial. But an affordance of algorithms is that they can be programmed to meet a variety of goals, and their speed and computing power might be put to work to achieve aims like maximizing diversity and chance encounters, rather than increasing profits, clicks, or views (Smith, 2019, pp. 290–291). This, also, is an avenue for future research.

Algorithms are becoming integral to the way we live our lives, including how we buy and sell books. What has emerged in this final section is an attempt to determine who should take responsibility for the multiple and often unforeseen consequences of selling books with algorithms: Amazon? Users? Governments?

This concept of responsibility is human. Bookselling algorithms cannot consider or follow up on the ethical implications of their recommendations. Although programmers might see what they are doing as a sort of pastoral custodianship, algorithms cannot take care with their recommendations (Bhaskar, 2016, pp. 229–230). Taking as much care with how we talk about algorithms – the power we attribute to them and the decisions we let them make for us – as we do about books should be part of bookselling discussions in the future.

References

Alharthi, H., Inkpen, D., and Szpakowicz, S. (2018) 'A Survey of Book Recommender Systems', *Journal of Intelligent Information Systems: Integrating Artificial Intelligence and Database Technologies*, 51(1), pp. 139–160.

Althoff, S. (2016) 'Algorithms Could Save Book Publishing – But Ruin Novels', *Wired*, 16 September. www.wired.com/2016/09/bestseller-code/. (Accessed: 8 April 2023).

Amrollahi, A., and McBride, N. (2019) 'How to Burst the Bubble in Social Networks?: 24th UK Academy for Information Systems (UKAIS) International Conference', *UKAIS 2019*, pp. 667–676.

Ananny, M. (2016) 'Toward an Ethics of Algorithms: Convening, Observation, Probability, and Timeliness', *Science, Technology, & Human Values*, 41(1), pp. 93–117.

Anderson, C. (2008a) 'The End of Theory: The Data Deluge Makes the Scientific Method Obsolete', *Wired*. www.wired.com/2008/06/pb-theory/. (Accessed: 22 May 2023).

Anderson, C. (2008b) *The Long Tail: Why the Future of Business Is Selling Less of More*. New York: Hyperion.

Austin, J. L. (1981) *How to Do Things with Words*. Oxford: Oxford University Press.

Beer, D. (2017) 'The Social Power of Algorithms', *Information, Communication & Society*, 20(1), pp. 1–13. https://doi.org/10.1080/1369118X.2016.1216147.

Berglund, K. (2021) 'Introducing the Beststreamer: Mapping Nuances in Digital Book Consumption at Scale', *Publishing Research Quarterly*, 37, pp. 135–151. https://doi.org/10.1007/s12109-021-09801-0.

Bezos, J. (1997) 'Amazon.com 1997 Shareholder Letter'. https://media.corporate-ir.net/media_files/irol/97/97664/reports/Shareholderletter97.pdf.

Bezos, J. (2021) '2020 Letter to Shareholders'. www.aboutamazon.com/news/company-news/2020-letter-to-shareholders. (Accessed: 2 June 2023).

Bhaskar, M. (2016) *Curation: The Power of Selection in a World of Excess*. London: Piatkus.

Bhaskar, M. (2020) 'AI and Publishing: What Next?', *Logos*, 31(3), pp. 13–19. https://doi.org/10.1163/18784712-03103003.

Blueprint for an AI Bill of Rights. (no date) *The White House*. www.whitehouse.gov/ostp/ai-bill-of-rights/. (Accessed: 7 June 2023).

Bookshop.org (no date) *About Us*, *Bookshop.org*. https://bookshop.org/info/about-us. (Accessed: 7 June 2023).

Borges, J. L. (2007[1941]) 'The Library of Babel', in D. A. Yates and J. E. Irby (eds.) *Labyrinths: Selected Stories & Other Writings*. New York: New Directions, pp. 51–58.

Bridle, J. (2018) *New Dark Age: Technology and the End of the Future*. London: Verso.

'browse, v.' (2016) *OED Online*. Oxford University Press. www.oed.com/view/Entry/23882. (Accessed: 31 May 2023).

Brynjolfsson, E., and Smith, M. D. (2003) 'Consumer Surplus in the Digital Economy: Estimating the Value of Increased Product Variety at Online Booksellers', *Management Science*, 49(11), pp. 1580–1596.

Bucher, T. (2018) *If . . . Then: Algorithmic Power and Politics*. New York: Oxford University Press.

Burrell, J. (2016) 'How the Machine "Thinks": Understanding Opacity in Machine Learning Algorithms', *Big Data & Society*, 3(1), pp. 1–10. https://doi.org/10.1177/2053951715622512.

Bury, L., and Kean, D. (2005) 'Browser to Buyer, Amazon Style: Amazon.co.uk Has Beat All Comers in the Battle of Online Book Sales', *The Bookseller*, 1 July, p. 26.

Carvajal, D. (1999) 'For Sale: Amazon.com's Recommendations to Readers', *The New York Times*, 8 February. https://archive.nytimes

.com/www.nytimes.com/library/tech/99/02/biztech/articles/08ama-zon.html. (Accessed: 4 August 2023).

de Certeau, M. (1988) *The Practice of Everyday Life*. Berkeley: University of California Press.

Chen, Y.-F. (2008) 'Herd Behavior in Purchasing Books Online', *Computers in Human Behavior*, 24(5), pp. 1977–1992.

Chen, L., Mislove, A. and Wilson, C. (2016) 'An Empirical Analysis of Algorithmic Pricing on Amazon Marketplace', in *Proceedings of the 25th International Conference on World Wide Web*. Republic and Canton of Geneva, CHE: International World Wide Web Conferences Steering Committee (WWW '16), pp. 1339–1349. Available at: https://doi.org/10.1145/2872427.2883089.

Cheney-Lippold, J. (2017) *We Are Data: Algorithms and the Making of Our Digital Selves*. New York: NYU Press.

Christin, A. (2022) *Metrics at Work: Journalism and the Contested Meaning of Algorithms*. Princeton: Princeton University Press.

Chun, W. H. K. (2008) *Control and Freedom: Power and Paranoia in the Age of Fiber Optics*. Cambridge, MA: The MIT Press.

Chun, W. H. K. (2018) 'Queerying Homophily', in C. Apprich, W. H. K Chun, F. Cramer, and H. Steyerl, *Pattern Discrimination*. Germany: Meson Press and University of Minnesota Press, pp. 59–98.

Cohn, J. (2019) *The Burden of Choice: Recommendations, Subversion, and Algorithmic Culture*. New Brunswick: Rutgers University Press.

Colbjørnsen, T. (2018) 'My Algorithm: User Perceptions of Algorithmic Recommendations in Cultural Contexts', in A. L. Guzman (ed.) *Human-Machine Communication: Rethinking Communication, Technology, and Ourselves*. New York: Peter Lang (Digital Formations, 117), pp. 167–183.

Cramer, F. (2018) 'Crapularity Hermeneutics: Interpretation as the Blind Spot of Analytics, Artificial Intelligence, and Other Algorithmic Producers of the Postapocalyptic Present', in C. Apprich, W. H. K Chun, F. Cramer, and

H. Steyerl, *Pattern Discrimination*. Germany: Meson Press and University of Minnesota Press, pp. 23–58.

Crawford, K. (2021) *Atlas of AI: Power, Politics, and the Planetary Costs of Artificial Intelligence*. New Haven: Yale University Press.

Dane, A. (2023) *White Literary Taste Production in Contemporary Book Culture*. Cambridge: Cambridge University Press. https://doi.org/10.1017/9781009234276.

Deutsch, J. (2022) *In Praise of Good Bookstores*. Princeton: Princeton University Press.

Dourish, P. (2016) 'Algorithms and Their Others: Algorithmic Culture in Context', *Big Data & Society*, 3(2), pp. 1–11. https://doi.org/10.1177/2053951716665128.

Eggers, D. (2013) *The Circle*. New York: Vintage Books.

Elkins, E. (2019) 'Algorithmic Cosmopolitanism: On the Global Claims of Digital Entertainment Platforms', *Critical Studies in Media Communication*, 36(4), pp. 376–389.

Evans, W. (2019) *Ruthless Quotas at Amazon Are Maiming Employees*, *The Atlantic*. www.theatlantic.com/technology/archive/2019/11/amazon-warehouse-reports-show-worker-injuries/602530/. (Accessed: 17 May 2023).

Finn, E. (2012) 'New Literary Cultures: Mapping the Digital Networks of Toni Morrison', in A. Lang (ed.) *From Codex to Hypertext: Reading at the Turn of the Twenty-first Century*. Amherst: University of Massachusetts Press, pp. 177–202.

Fletcher, A. (2021) 'Why Computers Will Never Read (or Write) Literature: A Logical Proof and Narrative', *Narrative*, 29(1), pp. 1–28.

Forsyth, M. (2014) *The Unknown Unknown: Bookshops and the Delight of Not Getting What You Wanted*. London: Icon Books.

Fuller, D., and Sedo, D. R. (2023) *Reading Bestsellers: Recommendation Culture and the Multimodal Reader*. Cambridge: Cambridge University Press. https://doi.org/10.1017/9781108891042.

Galloway, A. R. (2006) *Gaming: Essays on Algorithmic Culture*. Minneapolis: University of Minnesota Press.

Galloway, A. (2021) *Uncomputable: Play and Politics in the Long Digital Age*. Brooklyn: Verso.

Geissler, H. (2018) *Seasonal Associate*. Translated by K. Derbyshire. South Pasadena: Semiotext(e).

Gillespie, T. (2014) *The Relevance of Algorithms*. Cambridge, MA: The MIT Press.

Gillespie, T. (2016) 'Algorithm', in B. Peters (ed.) *Digital Keywords*. Princeton: Princeton University Press, pp. 18–30.

Greco, A. N. (2019) 'Economics of Publishing', in A. Phillips and M. Bhaskar (eds.) *The Oxford Handbook of Publishing*. Oxford: Oxford University Press, pp. 165–187.

Guendelsberger, E. (2019) *On the Clock: What Low-Wage Work Did to Me and How It Drives America Insane*. New York: Little, Brown.

Hallinan, B., and Striphas, T. (2016) 'Recommended for You: The Netflix Prize and the Production of Algorithmic Culture', *New Media & Society*, 18(1), pp. 117–137.

Havens, T. J. (2020) 'Algorithmic Audience Modeling and the Fate of African American Audiences', *Journal of Cinema and Media Studies*, 60(1), pp. 158–162.

Hennessey, A. (2000) 'Online Bookselling', *Publishing Research Quarterly*, 16(2), pp. 34–51. https://doi.org/10.1007/s12109-000-0005-9.

Horkheimer, M., and Adorno, T. W. (2002) *Dialectic of Enlightenment: Philosophical Fragments*. Edited by G. Schmid Noerr. Translated by E. Jephcott. Stanford: Stanford University Press.

Jarrett, K. (2022) *Digital Labor*. Cambridge: Polity.

Joque, J. (2022) *Revolutionary Mathematics: Artificial Intelligence, Statistics and the Logic of Capitalism*. London: Verso.

Kaiser, J., and Rauchfleisch, A. (2020) 'Birds of a Feather Get Recommended Together: Algorithmic Homophily in YouTube's Channel

Recommendations in the United States and Germany', *Social Media + Society*, 6(4), pp. 1–15. https://doi.org/10.1177/2056305120969914.

King, A. (2019) 'Publishing and Marketing', in B. Berensmeyer, G. Buelens, and M. Demoor (eds.) *The Cambridge Handbook of Literary Authorship*. Cambridge: Cambridge University Press, pp. 415–428.

Kirschenbaum, M. G. (2021) *Bitstreams: The Future of Digital Literary Heritage*. Philadelphia: University of Pennsylvania Press.

Kitchin, R. (2017) 'Thinking Critically about and Researching Algorithms', *Information, Communication & Society*, 20(1), pp. 14–29. https://doi.org/10.1080/1369118X.2016.1154087.

Knotzer, N. (2008) *Product Recommendations in E-Commerce Retailing Applications*. Peter Lang GmbH (Forschungsergebnisse der Wirtschaftsuniversität Wien: 17).

Laing, A., and Royle, J. (2013) 'Bookselling Online: An Examination of Consumer Behaviour Patterns', *Publishing Research Quarterly*, 29(2), pp. 110–127. https://doi.org/10.1007/s12109-013-9318-3.

Lamdan, S. (2022) *Data Cartels: The Companies That Control and Monopolize Our Information*. Stanford: Stanford University Press.

Mager, A. (2012) 'Algorithmic Ideology: How Capitalist Society Shapes Search Engines', *Information, Communication & Society*, 15(5), pp. 769–787. https://doi.org/10.1080/1369118X.2012.676056.

Marcus, J. (2010) *Amazonia: Five Years at the Epicenter of the Dot.com Juggernaut*. New York: The New Press.

Marketline (2022) 'Barnes & Noble, Inc. SWOT Analysis'.

Marketline (2023) 'Amazon.com, Inc. SWOT Analysis'.

McGurl, M. (2016) 'Everything and Less: Fiction in the Age of Amazon', *Modern Language Quarterly*, 77(3), pp. 447–471.

McGurl, M. (2021a) *Everything and Less: The Novel in the Age of Amazon*. London: Verso.

McGurl, M. (2021b) 'Unspeakable Conventionality: The Perversity of the Kindle', *American Literary History*, 33(2), pp. 394–415.

Miller, L. J. (2006) *Reluctant Capitalists: Bookselling and the Culture of Consumption*. Chicago: University of Chicago Press.

Miller, L. J. (2011) 'Perpetual Turmoil: Book Retailing in the Twenty-First Century United States', *LOGOS: The Journal of the World Book Community*, 22(3), pp. 16–25. https://doi.org/10.1163/095796511X604656.

Miller, L. J. (2013) 'Whither the Professional Book Publisher in an Era of Distribution on Demand', in A. N. Valdivia and V. Mayer (eds.) *The International Encyclopedia of Media Studies: Media Production*. Malden: Wiley-Blackwell, pp. 171–191.

Milliot, J. (2011) 'Acting on Impulse', *Publisher's Weekly*, 23 May. www.publishersweekly.com/pw/by-topic/industry-news/bookselling/article/47383-acting-on-impulse.html. (Accessed: 1 April 2023).

Murphy, A., and Contreras, I. (2022) *The Global 2000*, Forbes. www.forbes.com/lists/global2000/. (Accessed: 23 May 2023).

Murray, S. (2018) *The Digital Literary Sphere: Reading, Writing, and Selling Books in the Internet Era*. Baltimore: Johns Hopkins University Press.

Murray, S. (2021) 'Secret Agents: Algorithmic Culture, Goodreads and Datafication of the Contemporary Book World', *European Journal of Cultural Studies*, 24(4), pp. 970–989.

Nancy, J.-L. (2009) *On the Commerce of Thinking: Of Books & Bookstores*. Translated by D. Wills. New York: Fordham University Press. https://doi.org/10.5422/fso/9780823230365.001.0001.

Noble, S. U. (2018) *Algorithms of Oppression: How Search Engines Reinforce Racism*. New York: NYU Press.

O'Neil, C. (2016) *Weapons of Math Destruction: How Big Data Increases Inequality and Threatens Democracy*. New York: Crown.

O'Shea, L. (2019) *Future Histories: What Ada Lovelace, Tom Paine, and the Paris Commune Can Teach Us about Digital Technology*. London: Verso.

Packer, G. (2014) 'Cheap Words', *The New Yorker*, 9 February. www.newyorker.com/magazine/2014/02/17/cheap-words. (Accessed: 16 August 2022).

Pariser, E. (2012) *The Filter Bubble: How the New Personalized Web Is Changing What We Read and How We Think*. London: Penguin Books.

Pasquale, F. (2016) *The Black Box Society: The Secret Algorithms That Control Money and Information*. Cambridge, MA: Harvard University Press.

Petre, C., Duffy, B. E., and Hund, E. (2019) '"Gaming the System": Platform Paternalism and the Politics of Algorithmic Visibility', *Social Media + Society*, 5(4), pp. 1–11. https://doi.org/10.1177/2056305119879995.

Pressman, J. (2020) *Bookishness: Loving Books in a Digital Age*. New York: Columbia University Press.

Raley, R., and Rhee, J. (2023) 'Critical AI: A Field in Formation', *American Literature*, 95(2), pp. 185–204.

Ramone, J. (2020) *Postcolonial Literatures in the Local Literary Marketplace*. London: Palgrave MacMillan.

Richardson, R. (2021) 'Defining and Demystifying Automated Decision Systems', *Maryland Law Review* [Preprint]. https://ssrn.com/abstract=3811708. (Accessed: 2 May 2022).

Romano, B. (2019) 'Amazon Opens 4-Star Store at Seattle Headquarters as Online Giant Grows Physical Shopping Presence', *The Seattle Times*, 15 August. www.seattletimes.com/business/amazon/amazon-opens-4-star-store-at-seattle-headquarters-as-online-giant-grows-physical-shopping-presence/. (Accessed: 26 March 2023).

Seaver, N. (2017) 'Algorithms as Culture: Some Tactics for the Ethnography of Algorithmic Systems', *Big Data & Society*, 4(2), pp. 1–12. https://doi.org/10.1177/2053951717738104.

Seaver, N. (2022) *Computing Taste: Algorithms and the Makers of Music Recommendation*. Chicago: University of Chicago Press.

Sheff, D. (2000) *Interview with Jeff Bezos, David Sheff*. www.davidsheff.com/jeff-bezos. (Accessed: 25 August 2022).

Smith, R. E. (2019) *Rage Inside the Machine: The Prejudice of Algorithms, and How to Stop the Internet Making Bigots of Us All*. London: Bloomsbury.

Squires, C. (2020) 'The Global Market 1970–2015', in S. Eliot and J. Rose (eds.) *A Companion to the History of the Book*. 2nd ed. New York: John Wiley, pp. 601–614.

Srinivasan, R. (2017) *Whose Global Village? Rethinking How Technology Shapes Our World*. New York: NYU Press.

Stauff, M., van Romondt Vis, P., and van Es, K. (2023) 'Coffee Roasters' Data Vernacular: On the Entanglement of Digital Data and Craft', in K. van Es and N. Verhoeff (eds.) *Situating Data: Inquiries in Algorithmic Culture*. Amsterdam: Amsterdam University Press, pp. 31–47.

Steiner, A. (2015) 'Selling Books and Digital Files: A Comparative Study of the Sales of Books and E-Books in Sweden', *Northern Lights: Film and Media Studies Yearbook*, 13, pp. 11–27. https://doi.org/10.1386/nl.13.1.11_1.

Steiner, A. (2017) 'Select, Display, and Sell: Curation Practices in the Bookshop', *Logos*, 28(4), pp. 18–31. https://doi.org/10.1163/1878-4712-111 12138.

Stone, B. (2013) *The Everything Store: Jeff Bezos and the Age of Amazon*. Little, New York: Brown.

Stone, B. (2021) *Amazon Unbound: Jeff Bezos and the Invention of a Global Empire*. New York: Simon & Schuster.

Striphas, T. (2010) 'The Abuses of Literacy: Amazon Kindle and the Right to Read', *Communication and Critical Cultural Studies*, 7(3), pp. 297–317.

Striphas, T. (2015) 'Algorithmic Culture', *European Journal of Cultural Studies*, 18(4–5), pp. 395–412.

Striphas, T. (2023) *Algorithmic Culture before the Internet*. New York: Columbia University Press.

Sumpter, D. (2018) *Outnumbered: From Facebook and Google to Fake News and Filter-bubbles – The Algorithms That Control Our Lives*. London: Bloomsbury Sigma.

Tella, A., Uwaifo, S. O., and Akande, S. O. (2021) 'Patronage of Online Bookstores by Postgraduate Students at Nigerian Universities', *Mousaion*, 39(1), pp. 1–19. https://doi.org/10.25159/2663-659X/8062.

Thomas, N. P. (2019) 'Bookselling', in A. Phillips and M. Bhaskar (eds) *The Oxford Handbook of Publishing*. Oxford: Oxford University Press, pp. 398–408. Available at: https://doi.org/10.1093/oxfordhb/97801987 94202.013.20.

Thompson, J. B. (2010) *Merchants of Culture*. New York: Penguin.

Thompson, J. B. (2021) *Book Wars: The Digital Revolution in Publishing*. Cambridge: Polity.

Tolentino, J. (2017) 'Amazon's Brick-and-Mortar Bookstores Are Not Built for People Who Actually Read', *The New Yorker*, 30 May. www.newyorker.com/culture/cultural-comment/amazons-brick-and-mortar-bookstores-are-not-built-for-people-who-actually-read. (Accessed: 9 April 2023).

Vaidhyanathan, S. (2011) *The Googlization of Everything*. Berkeley: University of California Press.

van der Tuin, I. (2023) 'How Eva Louise Young (1861–1939) Found Me: On the Performance of Metadata in Knowledge Production', in K. van Es and N. Verhoeff (eds.) *Situating Data: Inquiries in Algorithmic Culture*. Amsterdam: Amsterdam University Press, pp. 189–206.

Walsh, M., and Antoniak, M. (2021) 'The Goodreads "Classics": A Computational Study of Readers, Amazon, and Crowdsourced Amateur Criticism', *Journal of Cultural Analytics*, 4, pp. 243–287.

Wiener, N. (1989) *The Human Use of Human Beings: Cybernetics and Society*. London: Free Association Books.

Yunkai, Z., and Wei, L. (2017) 'The Online Bookstore', *MATEC Web of Conferences*, 100. https://doi.org/10.1051/matecconf/201710002045.

Zhu, D. H., Wang, Y. W., and Chang, Y. P. (2018) 'The Influence of Online Cross-Recommendation on Consumers' Instant Cross-Buying Intention', *Internet Research*, 28(3), pp. 604–622. https://doi-org.proxy006.nclive.org/10.1108/IntR-05-2017-0211.

Zuboff, S. (2019) *The Age of Surveillance Capitalism: The Fight for a Human Future at the New Frontier of Power*. New York: PublicAffairs.

Cambridge Elements ☰

Publishing and Book Culture

SERIES EDITOR

Samantha Rayner

University College London

Samantha Rayner is Professor of Publishing and Book Cultures
at UCL. She is also Director of UCL's Centre for Publishing,
co-Director of the Bloomsbury CHAPTER (Communication
History, Authorship, Publishing, Textual Editing and
Reading) and co-Chair of the Bookselling Research Network.

ASSOCIATE EDITOR

Leah Tether

University of Bristol

Leah Tether is Professor of Medieval Literature and Publishing
at the University of Bristol. With an academic background in
medieval French and English literature and a professional
background in trade publishing, Leah has combined her
expertise and developed an international research profile in
book and publishing history from manuscript to digital.

ABOUT THE SERIES

This series aims to fill the demand for easily accessible, quality texts available for teaching and research in the diverse and dynamic fields of Publishing and Book Culture. Rigorously researched and peer-reviewed Elements will be published under themes, or 'Gatherings'. These Elements should be the first check point for researchers or students working on that area of publishing and book trade history and practice: we hope that, situated so logically at Cambridge University Press, where academic publishing in the UK began, it will develop to create an unrivalled space where these histories and practices can be investigated and preserved.

Cambridge Elements ☰

Publishing and Book Culture

Bookshops and Bookselling

Gathering Editor: Eben Muse

Eben Muse is Senior Lecturer in Digital Media at Bangor University and co-Director of the Stephen Colclough Centre for the History and Culture of the Book. He studies the impact of digital technologies on the cultural and commercial space of bookselling, and he is part-owner of a used bookstore in the United States.

ELEMENTS IN THE GATHERING

Printed in the United States
by Baker & Taylor Publisher Services